This Is Our Calling

This Is Our Calling

Edited by
Charles Richardson

First published in Great Britain in 2004 by
Society for Promoting Christian Knowledge
36 Causton Street
London SW1P 4ST
www.spckpublishing.co.uk

British Library Cataloguing-in-Publication Data
A catalogue record for this book is available from the British Library

ISBN 978–0–281–05600–2

Typeset by Avocet Typeset, Chilton, Aylesbury, Bucks
First printed in Great Britain by MPG Books Ltd, Bodmin, Cornwall
Subsequently digitally printed in Great Britain

Produced on paper from sustainable forests

Contents

Notes on Contributors

The Revd Christopher Burke
Having worked in Japan, West Yorkshire and the North East, Chris is currently Rector of Stepney in the East End of London. He initially read for a degree in law before training for ordination at Ripon College, Cuddesdon and Tamil Nadu Theological Seminary. He is married to Helen, a GP in east London.

The Revd Justine Allain Chapman
After having spent 10 years as a parish priest, Justine Allain Chapman is now the Director of Mission and Pastoral Studies for the South East Institute of Theological Education. Before ordination she was head of Religious Education at a secondary school in north London. Her interests are in interfaith relationships, liturgy and practical theology. Justine is a member of the General Synod of the Church of England. She is married to Thomas and they have three children.

The Venerable Stephen Conway
Stephen Conway has served for 16 years in the Diocese of Durham, where he has been, among other things, a parish priest and the Director of Ordinands. He is now Archdeacon of Durham and Canon Treasurer of Durham Cathedral. He was Chairman of the Executive of Affirming Catholicism from 1997 to 2003. He also belongs to the Society of Catholic Priests (SCP) and is a member of the Vocations Group which both sponsor. He acts as spiritual director to a number of priests and lay people.

The Revd Peter Edwards

Peter Edwards was ordained in 1985 following 11 years of teaching English in secondary schools. He has served in three parishes in the Diocese of Southwark, most recently as Rector of St Mary's, Newington in south central London from 1997. When asked if he was a late vocation, he always replies that he was a late response, having become aware at the age of 16 that God wanted him to be a priest, but that he wanted to be a teacher. He admits to ducking and diving from his vocation to the ordained ministry for some 15 years, before giving in gracefully. Peter was a founder member of the Society of Catholic Priests, is a past Rector of the Southwark SCP chapter where the Society began, and is a past spiritual director of Southwark Cursillo.

The Revd Stephen Ferns

Stephen currently works with the Ministry Division of the Archbishops' Council as a Bishops' Selection Conference Secretary and as the Vocations Officer for the Church of England. Previously, he was a curate and an incumbent on Teesside, a university chaplain at Durham University, and latterly Chaplain to the Bishop of Blackburn.

Sister Judith Gray, CSC

Sister Judith is a member of the Anglican Religious Community of the Sisters of the Church whose Mother House is at Ham Common, Richmond, Surrey and which has houses in Australia, Canada and the Solomon Islands as well as the UK. She trained as a teacher, studied theology and taught for some years (notably in Liverpool), before embarking on administrative and pastoral work and adult teaching within the Community and in a variety of ways outside it. In recent years she gained an MA in Christian Spirituality from Heythrop College, and is particularly interested in the interface between psychology and theology, not least as it affects current trends in spirituality. Born in Sydney, she is widely read and travelled.

The Revd Sheila Nunn

After teaching for 15 years, the late Sheila Nunn became a priest in her forties and was the incumbent of St James', Finchampstead, a semi-rural church in Berkshire. She had a particular interest in liturgy and was studying part-time for an MA in pastoral liturgy. Her vision led Sheila to encourage many to discover God's love.

The Revd Charles Richardson (Editor)

Charles Richardson, ordained in 1979, has been involved in vocational work for the whole of his ministry. After two curacies he spent five years as a Selection Secretary and Vocations Adviser at the Ministry Division. As Rector and Rural Dean of Hastings he continued to offer vocational advice and on his appointment as Vicar of St John's, East Dulwich, he became Vocations Adviser for the Woolwich Area in the Diocese of Southwark. He is a Pastoral Selector for Bishops' Selection Conferences.

The Revd Kevin Scully

Kevin Scully was born in Australia where he grew up and was educated. His family, involved in the local church, sent him to church schools but he turned from the Church and faith to earn a living as a journalist, writer and actor. After his marriage, serious illness and a move to England – but not necessarily because of them – he drifted back to the Church where he found himself exploring an earlier rejected call to priesthood. He bit the bullet and tested the call. He was ordained in 1993 and has since served in a number of churches in inner London. He is the author of ten produced stage works, two broadcast radio plays, two books, *Sensing the Passion* and *Women on the Way*, and was on the editorial panel of the Churches Together in Britain and Ireland Lent book, *Called to be Saints*.

The Revd David Stephenson

David Stephenson is a parish priest serving two urban estate parishes in Stockton-on-Tees in the Diocese of Durham where he is also a Vocations Adviser. David is Rector of the SCP Chapter in Durham. He came to faith through a Baptist church in Somerset in his late teens and became an Anglican while at university, rejoicing in a discovery of liturgy, spirituality and social engagement. David trained at Cranmer Hall in Durham and loves the North East. He is married with three young children.

Foreword

'Calling' is still a word that can induce a bit of panic in people. Perhaps you find it difficult to believe in a God who actually, concretely summons people to do things, in the way the Bible stories seem to take for granted. Isn't it on a level with hearing voices, or, indeed, speaking with tongues? The type of thing that modern Anglicans of the right sort don't really approve of? Or perhaps you do believe in a God who calls you personally to a unique task; but what if you get it wrong? Or what if circumstances seem to stand in the way of fulfilling this urgent and clear imperative?

The truth is that if we're going to talk about calling in the Church we need to put it into the context of our whole theology of creation and redemption. Certainly we need to shed some of our nervousness about the idea that God has a real personal purpose for our lives; equally we need to shed the fears that arise from seeing this as an inflexible demand, unrelated to who and where we are. And we shall only manage this if we have a wider canvas to contemplate, on which we can see something of the nature of the God with whom we have to do, and something of the nature of the humanity he has called to serve him and to rejoice in him.

The great strength of this little book is that it provides just this, a wide canvas, on which the great themes of Christian doctrine and the great narrative patterns of the Bible are spread out, to show how significant this language of calling is in a context in which God can be seen as constantly and passionately drawing us into life in the company of Jesus. It tells us very firmly that what God basically wants is for us to be ourselves – but that learning to be yourself is hard work, which you can only carry through by the most sustained and selfless listening.

So we are encouraged here to work at becoming real, in prayer and thinking, love and labour and self-discovery.

Of course the Church is in desperate need of people who are eager to answer God's call; but we shall have it very wrong if we think of this as a programme of recruitment to a clerical profession. The desperate need is for people who really and seriously ask how what God has given to them can be shared with and in Christ's Body; people who know enough about themselves to see the risks (and the awful comedy and tragedy) of trying to serve God in ministry, and who still want to know how they will be freed to give, trusting the Giver more than themselves. I hope that these pages will help to stir up more and more people who want to know this, and who are prepared to think through the often odd and always challenging possible answers.

And perhaps even more, I hope that the Church at large will be free to have a proper conversation about these things. Our ideas about ministry, including full-time paid ministry, are going into the melting-pot. We are less and less likely to see anything like a production-line of 'vicars' emerging out of discussions of vocation. The new sorts of Christian community that are developing around us will require new styles of ministerial service – and one of the convictions of the Catholic tradition is that the historic threefold pattern of ordained ministry is (surprisingly?) more receptive to some of this new thinking than various models based on definitions of professional life in this or that era or context.

So this book should be part of the lively discussion that is beginning afresh in the Church of England about its forms and structures. But it reminds us that all such discussion has to be anchored firmly in what we have come to know about the nature and the work of our God; only in that light do we come to know who we are and what we have. This is, rightly, a book that is essentially about wisdom and discernment, discovery of what matters most to us in the presence of God. So: read and discover.

Rowan Williams

Acknowledgement

The compilers and publishers gratefully acknowledge permission to reproduce copyright material in this book. Every effort has been made to trace and contact the copyright owners. If there are any inadvertent omissions in the acknowledgements we apologize to those concerned.

Introduction

Charles Richardson

A voice from God

Many things unite us as human beings. Chief among them
is that we are all called to be children of God and are
created in his image. This book has been written especially
for those who are exploring a sense of call, and who want
to look at their lives and future in vocational terms; those
who want to trust the Creator for the journey, and who
want to find out more about what he is calling them to do
and be. It will be particularly helpful for those considering
ordination or other forms of authorized ministry.

Down the ages, even ideas about matters as profound as
the origins of the world have guided the actions and
destinies of men and women. They believe that the God
whose voice brought the universe to birth still speaks
powerfully, mysteriously and insistently in their lives. Many
believe that this 'voice', enlivened by the scriptures and
liturgies of the Church, continues to make itself known. It
is heard by many who are searching for answers, treading
carefully an unknown path, or attempting to find a way that
is in accord with the life of God found in Jesus Christ.

Some have led their entire lives attuned to this voice and
are as clear as human beings can be that the steps to be
taken, the decisions already made, are in response to the
'voice within' that they have heard – however this may be
described or understood. There are others who, from time
to time, have encountered a maze which no human advice
or mind can hope to unravel. Yet in the midst of confusion
and doubt they are prompted by some energy which leads

them to take a particular course and which they may describe afterwards as being the action of the Holy Spirit. There are others still. They have led lives of sacrifice and prayer, and their whole *raison d'être* appears to be focused on listening out for a word from God. Yet they would claim never to have heard such a voice or felt such an impulse. They remain committed to the journey because they trust that God is there, even though no call, no suggestion has come to them directly.

The 'voice of God within' is being heard, but as variously as our personalities, cultures and situations will allow. Describing this 'voice' or 'call' from God is a metaphor for the many ways in which we experience the things of God. *This Is Our Calling* is designed for all who find themselves to be disciples in the Church, and perhaps for those who do not feel that they belong to any Christian denomination. The journey described here is not one which needs to be undertaken alone, or in solitude; the quietness which enables us to listen will have a vital place in our ways of discovery but these chapters will unfurl more fully and colourfully if such explorations are engaged with as part of a small discussion group. Each chapter has a particular vocational theme and each provides various avenues to explore and questions to discuss. There should usually be a place for quiet reflection within the group and again this is provided for.

But one premise lies behind both explorations of trust and call. 'Calls' are part of life and they always have been. We are called upon daily to help others and we call out our greetings across the street or in the supermarket. Electronic messages and calls are so much part of life that we are often confused and frightened by the demands they make on us. 'There's a call for you' is a phrase we have all heard and the words have lifted our hearts or contracted our brows. 'There's a call for you' is a declaration that something in this exploration is for *you*. We hope that these chapters will enable you to hear that God has something to say to you about your future, the way your discipleship might develop, and perhaps even how you may need to pause and change direction.

When Affirming Catholicism and the Society of Catholic Priests decided to work together to prepare this volume we wondered who might find it most useful. We wanted to help those who had come to a crossroad, or even a breathing space, in their lives; who were considering their discipleship and their future. We were inspired by *This Is Our Faith*,[1] and this book can be seen as a companion to it. As that publication explores the origins and development of faith as experienced in the Anglican tradition so we hope that this book will enable many to explore how God's voice has been heard in the past and how it might guide us for the future.

Centring on the theme of vocation, these essays discuss various aspects in the light of the Catholic Anglican tradition in today's world. The authors are (almost) all parish priests in this tradition and write out of their experience as well as their theological understanding.

Charles Richardson

A prayer of Thomas Merton

God we have no idea where we are going. We do not see the road ahead of us. We cannot know for certain where it will end. Nor do we really know ourselves, and the fact that we think we are following your will does not mean that we are actually doing so.

But we believe that the desire to please you does in fact please you. And we hope that we have that desire in all that we are doing. We hope that we will never know anything apart from that desire. And we know that if we do this you will lead us by the right road, though we may know nothing about it.

Therefore we will trust always though we may seem to be lost and in the shadow of death. We will not fear, for you are ever with us, and you will never leave us to face our perils alone.[2]

CHAPTER 1

The Call through Creation

Charles Richardson

God calls his world — with everything and everyone in it — into relationship with him. It is within his world that we find our purpose, and our vocation. We co-create with God in all our discipleship and all our activities.

We live in a world which is as beautiful as it is confusing. We experience its power and danger as well as its poetic wonder. It is intricate and complicated; it is breathtaking in its scope and freedom.

Whatever we may think of ourselves, our world and our faith, it is clear that they cannot be separated. We belong here in this world and it is in this world at this time, and not any other, that we are called upon to live out our faith and respond to the demands which are made upon us.

We declare that this is God's world. That statement is very differently understood according to our theological tradition but it basically means that because we inhabit this world we belong to God and are responsible to God. It also means that we are part of the world as a whole and related to its other parts: we are neither above it nor detached from it. But God's relationship to this world is full of contradictions. God creates all there is for a specific purpose but that has not prevented either natural disaster or humanity's abuse of the natural order. If we wish to understand our own place in this world we need to consider how scripture has described God's relationship to the world we live in.

CHARLES RICHARDSON

Giving birth to a world: scripture and creation

Every story must begin somewhere. Our own human stories begin before the moment of our birth. We have a life, which has its origins beyond. Our story stretches back to our ancestors and reaches forward to the future. The scriptures, which testify to past and future, are simply a reflection of the story of the universe. The story of the world, its origins and destiny, is explored, interpreted and reinterpreted in the pages of the Bible.

The earliest summaries of faith found in the Bible do not primarily refer to God as creator. They tend to concentrate on God's mighty deeds in history; story after story is told to illustrate the fact that the God who showed power in history could also make the forces of nature serve his purpose. God prepared a path through the Red Sea, preserved the people of Israel in the wilderness and even rescued their armies (Judg. 5.20–1).

The beliefs that figure prominently in the religions of the Near East containing stories, images and myths about the creation of the world are reflected (but also much modified) in the faith of Judaism, which had its own ways of telling the story. There are several ways of describing God's relationship to creation, and two are found at the beginning of the Old Testament.

One story, called the Jahwist, is found in the second chapter of the Book of Genesis (vv. 4b–25) and perhaps dates back to the reign of King Solomon (962–922 BC). A parallel account, but more comprehensive and intense, is to be found in the preceding chapter of Genesis (1.1–2.3) which probably dates from the time of the Exile (600–500 BC) or later. These dates are contested and neither account is a literal attempt to explain the origin or evolution of nature. But, placed as they are at the very beginning of the Bible, they suggest that God's creation of the world is the starting point of all history – and the starting point of all our stories. Not only is it literally a starting point; more significantly (the physics are open to discussion and are not the main point of these texts) it is a claim about the world's constant relationship of dependence upon God.

In the biblical picture of that relationship, the creation of the world begins a series of covenants or commitments between God and the universe. God has a purpose, and the setting for that purpose is our world. God calls the world into being and all his subsequent calls are creative acts in which nature, communities and individuals are called into relationship with him. When the accounts of creation claim that 'God created the heavens and the earth' (Gen. 1.1) they are underlining that everything belongs to God simply because he has touched it and called it into being.

Despite the differences between the creation stories they agree in ascribing creation to the free and spontaneous initiative of God. This means that all God's subsequent relationships are similarly free and creative, and that his presence shapes and inspires all that occurs. God's action as creator also defines our responsibilities towards the universe and warns us against the threat of chaos and disorder. God, the creator of the universe, does not thereby free the world from risk and uncertainty. The development of all species presupposes that there is danger and the possibility of extinction, as well as the promise of glory. It is the freedom that makes the journey of our world so fragile, and miraculous, in its evolution.

These interpretations of creation are a poetic and theological way of understanding the origins of the world. There is also the way found in Proverbs 8.22ff. and Psalm 33.6, echoed in Sirach 24 and Wisdom of Solomon 9.1, whereby God creates by his wisdom; a poetic, yet reasoned, way of rejoicing in the complexity and wonder of the world's relationship with God.

> *Ever since the creation of the world his eternal power and divine nature, invisible though they are, have been understood and seen through the things he has made.*
>
> Romans 1.20

Christianity, in its many forms, affirms all this. Jesus refers to the creation of the world and in Pauline and Johannine thought Christ shares in all God's creative acts, from the beginning of the world to the end of all things. Each of the New Testament narratives shares the experience that Jesus, the Messiah, changed their view of everything. Involved in every part of creation Jesus fills all existence:

> *In the beginning was the Word, and the Word was with God, and the Word was God. He was in the beginning with God. All things came into being through him, and without him not one thing came into being.*
>
> John 1.1–3

He is included in every aspect of life because he is the clue to the meaning of life in all its dimensions. For the writers of the New Testament Jesus had to be identified with (indeed succeed or replace) not simply Israel, the Passover, the Law and the Temple but the whole of God's word and wisdom. Jesus was in the very shape and sense of everything.

So the thread of creativity that runs through the Bible has a point and a purpose. It is the invisible connection that unites the whole of our lives. If God has power and love enough to call us into being, he has given us power and love enough to fulfil his calling – within this world of ours.

Called to birth: creation and nature

Jesus' birth as a human baby, however strange and mysterious the events surrounding it, has been understood to imply an intimate connection or communion between God and the world. Jesus, as God's disclosure of himself, is born in human form and shares in the possibilities and limitations common to all humanity. The birth of such a child and his growth through puberty into adulthood implies his sharing in our characteristics. He breathed and shone and functioned and died as we all do. He cried out in ecstasy and in pain. He knew love and felt rejection. His own vocation will be explored later in Chapter Four, but for the moment we simply need to trust that there was some ultimate purpose in sending him as a human child.

Jesus' preaching and lifestyle reflected the world and age in which he lived. He saw that the changing seasons and the experience of daily life had their own story to tell about the links between the creation and every individual and community. He told stories that spoke of a Father's love and concern which were reflected in the natural order. Birth, illness, dying and the influence of evil were all dramatically presented in his parables, and in his power to heal and bring peace to troubled souls. The governing principle of Jesus' vocation was not theories about the creation of the world, but the desire and demand of his loving Father, experienced in the world. The world was significant because it was God's gift and was the context in which Jesus' obedience and sacrifice would be faced.

The world is significant because it is the place of both our natural and our spiritual birth. Very shortly after Jesus' death Paul was already speaking (about AD 55) of the new birth experienced by all believers. 'In Christ, there is a new creation' (2 Cor. 5.17). For Paul the world is touched, even sometimes possessed, by evil (Rom. 8.19–25), but just as Jesus' own birth into the natural world brought about a new beginning for humanity so within the created order can men and women live out a new kind of birth as disciples of Jesus. Christ is the firstborn of a new creation, a kind of new Adam (1 Cor. 15.22) and out of a natural birth a new birth is possible for all. Jesus is so revolutionary that we see him as if the creation of the human race were starting off all over again.

This new way of life, this new start, is experienced through forgiveness and a trust that there is a plan and a purpose for this world – and beyond. We are born afresh into a relationship with Christ, with one another and with our world. The processes of natural birth are wonderful, agonizing and full of potential. So it is with our new birth in Jesus Christ: it is as we are, newly born, that we are shaped and challenged for our own vocation and call as human beings belonging to God.

Called by name: lives in creation

> *Lift up your eyes on high and see:*
> *Who created these?*
> *He who brings out their host and numbers them,*
> *calling them all by name;*
> *because he is great in strength, mighty in power,*
> *not one is missing.*
>
> *Isaiah 40.26*

In the Old Testament 'calling' and 'creating' are very closely linked. In Isaiah 40.26 God creates the stars and calls them each by name. In the creation stories in Genesis we see a glimpse of God creating and naming all that is. The prophets of Israel remind their people that they too have been called by name (Isa. 43.1). The naming of stars, planets, plants and animals gives them a purpose, a place, a responsibility to and in the created order, and it means an intimacy of relationship. They are each called to BE, to exist, as themselves. They bear their name and answer the One who gave them each a distinct identity. As Archbishop Rowan Williams states in his publication for the Franciscans entitled *Vocation*,

> The act of creation can be seen as quite simply this, the vocation of things to be themselves, distinctive, spare and strange. God does not first create and then differentiate a great multitude of roles within creation: in one act he creates a multiple, noisy, jostling and diverse reality.[1]

> But now thus says the LORD,
>   he who created you, O Jacob,
>   he who formed you, O Israel:
> Do not fear, for I have redeemed you;
> I have called you by name, you are mine.
>   Isaiah 43.1

This theological understanding has found a place in one of the Eucharistic Prayers found in *The Book of Common Prayer* of the Episcopal Church of the USA:

> God of all power, Ruler of the Universe, you are worthy of glory and praise . . .
>
> At your command all things came to be: the vast expanse of interstellar space, galaxies, suns, the planets in their courses, and this fragile earth, our island home . . .
>
> From the primal elements you brought forth the human race, and blessed us with memory, reason and skill. You made us the rulers of creation. But we turned against you, and betrayed your trust; and we turned against one another . . .

> *Again and again you called us to return. Through prophets and sages*
> *you revealed your righteous Law. And in the fullness of time you sent*
> *your only Son, born of a woman, to fulfil your Law, to open for us the*
> *way of freedom and peace.* [2]

If all this is true of the stars in space then it is equally true of those who are humanly born into this great web of identity and promise. Each human being, however lost and forsaken many lives appear to be, is a unique and precious part of this great world.

> To be *is* to be where you are, who you are, and what you are – a person with a certain genetic composition, a certain social status, a certain set of capabilities. From the moment of birth (even from before that) onwards, you will be at each moment that particular bundle of conditioning and possibilities. And to talk about God as your creator means to recognize at each moment that it is his desire for you to be, and so his desire for you to be there as the person you are. It means he is calling you by your name, at each and every moment, wanting you to be you. [3]

Our vocation then, as human beings, does not simply happen out of the blue at a particular date and time. Even St Paul, who could date his conversion and call almost to the very minute, always spoke of being set apart from his mother's womb. Our vocation arises out of humanity and our humanity gives us a particular place in the world.

As *This Is Our Calling* develops it will be possible to see how our baptism and our baptismal naming give us the generating seed of our vocation which begins before we are born. The vocation of your own church community, as well as the wider Church, will have a place in your own vocation and you will have part in that wider calling. But this adventure will not be a tidy or straightforward journey: many events, surprises and burdens will both complicate and deepen our calling by God to be ourselves. This is all part of the journey we share with one another and with Jesus our brother. It is a story which was not ended by his death, and will not end with ours. The outworking of our vocation will take time and energy and conflicting calls will be part of that journey.

Conflicting calls: working things out in a real world

The creation story illustrates the reality of God's power, which enables order to come from chaos. But the chaotic power inherent in the world is still felt in the events of the natural, as well as the human, world.

> In the beginning when God created the heavens and the earth, the earth was a formless void and darkness covered the face of the deep, while a wind from God swept over the face of the waters.
>
> Genesis 1.1–2

We live in a world in which the potential to do good and evil is equally possible. The outworking of our vocation is in the context of many and varying demands. God calls us at many levels. He calls creation, calls the Church, calls my congregation, and he calls me. He calls the entirety of our lives, through birth and death, and at specific times and places, he calls us to particular actions. This understanding leads us to feel that we may be guided or inspired to different ways of living. There is a variety of calls and no one call is inherently better or higher than any other. The call of a priest, monk or nun is not superior to the call of someone who designs a house, or cares for the sick or repairs a washing machine. God speaks to us through the language of everyday events. Each new moment or situation holds a clue to God's call and we will always find our call in the circumstances and experiences of daily life. Any matter, large or small, may relate to a call, and our vocation may not be so much a call to 'do' as to 'be'. The fact of our humanity and the many-threaded relationships which exist will lead us into recognizing how lightly we take some of our responsibilities and also how complicated is the network of relationships in which we find ourselves. If God is the originator of all, it will be clear that the fulfilment of each component part of the universe is his aim. His creative purpose is freely to allow the space necessary for each part to be itself. But the demands of a growing population are at variance with the needs of plants and animals for which we have been given responsibility. The complicated chain of events which links the destruction of rainforests in one part of the world to floods in another part of the globe alerts us to the myriad ways in which needs and responsibilities will clash. Our human existence and network of relationships alone will tell us that not everything or everyone, nor even every part of our individual selves, can be totally fulfilled at all times. Sister Catherine, CSC, of the Vocations Group, talks frankly about the complexities in discerning vocation:

> When we start to explore something that we have begun to consider as being part of our vocation, or calling from God, we may discover that there is much about it that contains what we do most deeply desire. It may not be the last thing on earth that we would consider, although for some it often is! There can be feelings of inadequacy for the task, which leaves plenty of room for God's grace to be at work in us. There is frequently a great deal of struggling, and it is often said, 'It won't go away'. However through our prayer, and not always swiftly, we do find a place of peace from which to respond to our calling. Initially as

we live out our calling we continue to struggle with the reality of it for us. Later when we might feel more established in our vocation we can still awake and say to ourselves, 'Am I really doing this?'

As well as being called to save and convert people into membership of the Church, we are called to a primary task of liberating people into the fullness of their own already-graced humanity and to revealing to others the blessedness of their very being. We are called upon to balance a re-emerging theology of creation with an understanding of revelation which honours the intrinsic goodness of all that God has made *and* to acknowledge the desperate need for redemption. In the miracle of human birth and existence the indelible character of the divine image can never be forgotten. A Christian theology of creation and incarnation holds strongly the view that we co-create with God in all our vocations, and sometimes like him must create purpose out of chaos. We need to supply what may be missing in making divine redemption and calling present among us today. God wished to create out of pure love and then in time to become that creation. That 'becoming' happened in Jesus Christ. In his life within us we are called to bring to birth the image of God in those around us. So our search to understand our own call must include the discernment of the calls of those around us, particularly those who are closest to us. This commitment to those we know is allied to a commitment to all humanity and alongside that comes a responsibility of caring for the earth itself. 'This too, is the body of God.'[4]

In 1835, Søren Kierkegaard (1813–55) wrote in his journal:

What I really lack is to be clear in my mind what I am to do, not what I am to know . . . The thing is to understand myself, to see what God really wishes me to do . . . What

good would it do me to be able to explain the meaning
of Christianity if it had no deeper significance for me and
for my life?'[5]

'*Live* the questions now,' urges Rainer Maria Rilke. 'Perhaps
then, someday far in the future, you will gradually, without
even noticing it, live your way into the answer.'[6]
    How can we hear this call? What could hearing it mean
as we live day by day? How can we help each other to hear
God's voice and follow where God leads? In the end
answers will emerge through the asking and answering of
questions. Understanding that God calls us to something,
and meeting with others for insight and support, helps us
to live out these questions. In this way we will gain hearts
that listen, and respond to God's gentle but insistent voice.

Some questions

1 How would you describe the vocation of your own local
  church community?
2 How would you unravel the conflicting demands of being
  a parent or a partner with the possibility of being called
  to a specific ministry?
3 How is it possible for our care of the earth to allow the
  various parts of the universe to find the fulfilment which
  God has willed for it since the beginning of time?

CHAPTER 2

The Call of a People

Justine Allain Chapman

Within the universe in which God delights there will always be those who respond to his creative love. In ages past, and in this age, people and communities have heard a voice which calls them to a special purpose or service.

Called to follow

The Hebrew scriptures are a record of the story of the people of Israel and their relationship with God. Throughout the pages God calls them into a relationship, making a covenant with them and reminding them to keep it. God calls the whole community, but how far the community responds depends upon whether individuals hear, respond and encourage others to hear and respond. In this chapter we shall see that God's call goes out to all creation and also to individuals and peoples. The call is dramatically heard by some, but inherited by others who then have to make it their own. Still today God's call is heard and people respond.

> *Now the LORD said to Abram, 'Go from your country and your kindred and your father's house to the land that I will show you. I will make you a great nation, and I will bless you, and make your name great, so that you will be a blessing. I will bless those who bless you, and the one who curses you I will curse; and in you all the families of the earth shall be blessed.'*
>
> Genesis 12.1–2

This part of the story begins with God calling an individual to leave his home country and family and travel into the unknown with the knowledge that God will bless him and make from him a great nation (Gen. 12.1–2). At this time there is no great community, just God's call to this one man. It is his response which brings the community into being.

His name is Abram, which is later to become Abraham, the father of many nations; for God's call is to expand and affect many others even though it begins with Abram. Abram, his wife Sarai (later Sarah) and nephew Lot set out with their possessions and this household does become a bigger family and eventually a nation. Whenever we answer God's call, it is never in isolation: God calls us right where we are to go to a new place, perhaps physically, certainly spiritually, and other people, whose lives are closely linked with ours, are affected by the relationship we have with God.

Abraham
The first patriarch, man of faith and obedient to God. Name means 'father of many nations'. Once known as Abram. Origins – Ur in Mesopotamia, then Haran in Northern Syria in third millennium BC. Husband of Sarah, uncle of Lot, father of Isaac and Ishmael and others. Called by a previously unknown God who promised him land and descendants to leave everything and travel to Canaan.

The Old Testament story is one of a relationship with a saving God and a rebellious people, but as individuals respond to God's call, others are able to trust God whatever is happening. The first patriarchs are Abraham, Isaac and Jacob, grandfather, father and son – the call comes to each of them personally and yet is somehow inherited. We find Jacob's family without enough food and so they all move to Egypt under the direction of Jacob's son Joseph who had been sold into slavery by his brothers, but had risen to power in Egypt.

Called to liberation

> Then the LORD said, 'I have observed the misery of my people who are in Egypt; I have heard their cry on account of their taskmasters. Indeed, I know their sufferings, and I have come down to deliver them from the Egyptians, and to bring them up out of that land to a good and broad land, a land flowing with milk and honey.'
>
> Exodus 3.7–8

For 400 years the Hebrews were slaves to the Egyptians. But at the beginning of the Book of Exodus God hears their cries (Exod. 3.7–8). When we are called, we are called from something and for something. We hear parents saying 'Come over here and have your lunch.' Abraham was called from Ur, in Babylonia. He was called to follow, to a future where there would be descendants and a land to live in. In the time of slavery in Egypt God's call was from slavery to freedom in the promised land. It was not really different from Abraham's call; the people had to follow as Abraham had to. Slaves have no future, nor land of their own, and God called them out of Egypt in order for them to have both.

A call to liberation is characteristic of God and we see it throughout history. Christians led the movement to abolish slavery in Great Britain in the eighteenth century, as well as the Civil Rights Movement in the United States. Christians were also heavily involved in the fight against apartheid. When history is written it is often one or two names we associate with what has happened – William Wilberforce with the abolition of slavery, Martin Luther King and Archbishop Desmond Tutu with racial equality. Many people, however, those with power and influence and those without, together respond to the call to bring about liberation.

One call, many responses

Moses was keeping the flock of his father-in-law Jethro, the priest of Midian; he led his flock beyond the wilderness, and came to Horeb, the mountain of God. There the angel of the LORD appeared to him in a flame of fire out of a bush; he looked, and the bush was blazing, yet it was not consumed. Then Moses said, 'I must turn aside and look at this great sight, and see why the bush is not burned up.' When the LORD saw that he had turned aside to see, God called to him out of the bush, 'Moses, Moses!' And he said, 'Here I am.'

Exodus 3.1–4

It can be easy for us to think that God just called Moses from the burning bush and that the people were freed. This is too simplistic a way of looking at the situation. God's voice at creation brought life into being and each human person is made in God's image. God's spirit moves across the earth, and stirs us up to respond to all that is of God. In the first chapters of Exodus we see many people responding to God's call to deliver those in slavery. Most of them act out of a deep sense of integrity, justice and compassion. Shiphrah and Puah were Hebrew midwives who were ordered to kill the baby boys that they delivered. 'But the midwives', we are told, 'feared God' (Exod. 1.17) and so they took part in non-confrontational and non-violent resistance. They let the boys live and made excuses to the Egyptians saying that the boys were born before they arrived. Shiphrah and Puah (along with Moses' mother and sister Miriam) worked with compassion and quick-wittedness towards saving and nurturing the lives of the next generation of Hebrews. They acted out of what they knew was right; they took risks that could have caused them their deaths; and they trusted in God for some good to come. God's call was in the air and deep within them; it always is, now as then. In many movements and events ever since similar things have happened. Rosa Parks, on 1 December 1955 in Montgomery, Alabama, refused to give up her seat on a bus to a white man who wanted it. By this simple act, she set in motion the American Civil Rights Movement, which led to the Civil Rights Act of 1964 and ultimately ensured that today all African Americans must be given equal treatment with whites under the law. Parks did not know that she was making history nor did she intend to do so; she simply knew that after a long day's work she did not want to move. Because of her fatigue but moreover because of her courage, America was changed for ever.

Rosa Parks

Born in 1913 in Tuskegee, Alabama. Worked as a seamstress and for the National Association for the Advancement of Colored People with her husband Raymond Parks. Greatest achievement — sparking the Civil Rights Movement in the US by refusing to give up her bus seat to a white passenger. Rosa was arrested and imprisoned for breaking the Montgomery segregation laws. This first public confrontation brought the name of Martin Luther King to the ears of America and a 381-day boycott of the city bus line. In 1956 the Supreme Court ruled that segregation was illegal on public buses. Rosa, a deaconess of her church, St Matthew's in Detroit, continued the fight for equal rights and treatment for African Americans.

The call of all

In the story of the Exodus there were others we might be surprised to find who responded to the call for freedom. Pharaoh's daughter had a part to play, for God calls us all of whatever religion or race to know his purposes and respond. Moses' call from the burning bush is the one we remember, but each person in the story responded to God's call. In doing so they offered who they were to bring about God's purposes.

Offering who we are includes whatever is in our past and present. Moses' past included education as an Egyptian and his experience of minding sheep. He had learned from his father-in-law Jethro, the priest of Midian, and from his own experience as a husband and father. This is used by God as Moses leads the people along with his experience as an escaped murderer. All these influences came together to make Moses the one most suited to negotiate with Pharaoh and lead the Hebrews out of slavery. He had fled before, been in the court before; now he would have to lead a wayward people as he had led the wayward sheep and teach the people about their God using much he had learned from Jethro.

God was calling human beings to respond to the cry of the Israelites for freedom: the call was heard and responded to in different ways by people who had very different parts to play. The call crossed racial and religious boundaries and was not without cost; but because it was heard, God moved among the people and brought about liberation.

The call heard from within and without

The call for liberation is still being heard. Abraham and Moses had very clear, dramatic calls. For Shiphrah and Puah the call was heard and answered from within their own knowledge of what was God's will. Some calls do not seem either to rise up from within or to be a direct experience of God, but are a call from the community, with God's undergirding.

When the people of Israel escaped from Egypt and entered the promised land there was an unsettled period, that of the judges, when the people became established in the land. They asked Samuel to make a king for them so that they could be like other successful nations, and reluctantly he anointed Saul. Later on, Samuel anointed David who was a young man and at the time had no prospect of being king because Saul was still reigning and had heirs. Neither Saul nor David felt called to this role: the call came through Samuel and the people of Israel. They had to accept the role and grow into an understanding of it as God's will for their lives.

There are circumstances when God's call comes through other people, as it did for David, and even sometimes seems impossible. It may not come in any dramatic way, but it can come to a person from the community because they have the right qualities for the task or because the potential is discerned. Many of those called in the Bible did not have dramatic experiences. Abraham was called, but his son Isaac and grandson Jacob inherited the role of patriarch, the one who was to take the Covenant down to future generations. The kings after David similarly inherited their role and needed to grow into an understanding and experience of it as being of God. Some, like Joshua and Elisha, took on the mantle of someone (Moses and Elijah for them) who had begun a task that needed to continue under a new person. God calls each of us and calls us all. The circumstances of our lives and the communities to which we belong shape that call.

The call to all

> I am the LORD,
> I have called you in righteousness,
> I have taken you by the hand and kept you.
> Isaiah 42.6

In the later history of the people of Israel the nation develops a sense of being called by God, of being chosen and privileged. This call comes with responsibility however – the responsibility to keep the Law and the Covenant and be a blessing to other nations. The prophet Isaiah preached that Israel must be a light to enlighten the nations (Isa. 42.6) and Jesus stood within this tradition which preached that God is continually calling and loves all people of every nation. God's call is for all creation and his people are to shine as lights in the world as the baptism service says. Jesus spoke of his disciples being the 'salt of the earth' and the 'light of the world' continuing the Old Testament tradition. The privilege of being called by God brings with it the responsibility of acknowledging God in all aspects of life. Old Testament prophets such as Amos and Micah emphasize the needs of the poor and the importance of social justice above religious ritual. God cares about the plight of all human beings. Every person is valuable, whatever their economic or social status, race or religion, and we are called to liberation and freedom for ourselves and others. God's people are called to enshrine such care for all nations in the ways they behave.

One book of the Bible which expresses God's concern for all the world is the Book of Jonah. In it we find the prophet Jonah refusing to go to a foreign city, to the people of Nineveh, to preach to them so that they would repent. We find that the sailors on the boat have more faith in Jonah's God than he does and that the people of Nineveh are only too willing to turn from their wicked ways. It is Jonah who is faithless and who needs the persuasion of the big fish to encourage him to obey God's call. The Book of Jonah, along with books like that of the Moabite woman Ruth, reminds us that God calls people from every race and religion to follow a particular way of life – a deep trust in God along with loving service of humanity.

> **Ruth**
>
> *A Moabite woman — a foreigner who shows loyalty and devotion. Widowed daughter-in-law of Naomi, an Israelite. Lived in time of constant famine, in the period of the judges c. 1200 BC. Wife of Boaz and great-grandmother of King David.*

We can wonder whether God is calling us. The answer is yes, for God calls all people as individuals and as nations and communities to life and to liberation. Each call can be experienced in a variety of ways, within and without, dramatic and inherited. As we respond we become lights for others to see who God is.

Some questions

1 How is your church calling people to take up particular tasks in the community of faith or wider community?
2 Where in your neighbourhood can you see signs of people responding to God's call to follow, serve or liberate?
3 How important is it to have a dramatic call to take a new direction in life?

CHAPTER 3

The Call for Others

Stephen Conway

Already with our sights on Jesus we see some of his saints through his eyes. We watch the ways in which utterly different men and women respond to the call of the one who created them. In the light of Jesus' own vocation we can see the vocational lives of those who, as we try to, are responding to something within them. This is an exciting and often searing journey in which we find ourselves refined by nothing less than the grace of God and the communion we have with all the saints. Our calling, whatever it might be, will involve being called for the sake of others.

The vision of God and the pattern of Christ

Any working out of any calling has to be rooted in our vision of, and relationship with, our Creator, Saviour and Sanctifier. Many people sense a vocation to serve humanity in costly ways and pursue it without any explicit faith in God. In the Gospel Jesus teaches us that our love for our neighbour begins in our recognition of the holiness of God.

God invites us to share in his holiness and we can be holy only in terms of how fully we respond. We are saved by grace through the cross, and by this participation in the divine life we are sanctified by the power of God's Spirit. Any calling which enables us to look out to the world needs to be grounded in our longing for the God who is always moving out towards us, always seeking deeper relationship with us, always beckoning us into new possibility. In this relationship we can become the people we are meant to be and can find our potential strength in our vulnerability. The God whom we seek to serve is the One whose nature is already to be fully poured out for the flourishing of the whole of creation. This generous God has made us by grace, has called us through Christ and commissions us in the power of the Spirit to serve that same flourishing.

> *The glory that you have given me I have given them, so that they may be one, as we are one, I in them and you in me, that they may become completely one, so that the world may know that you have sent me and have loved them even as you have loved me.*
>
> John 17.22–3

We are ignited for that service by the fire of God's glory. Our vocation is real only if we experience the world shot through with the glory of the life of God. The spring of our service of this glory is our worship in which by Word and Sacrament we celebrate the glory of the God who loves and saves the universe. We come in penitence seeking that grace and mercy by which we shall be transformed into the likeness of the glorified humanity of Christ. In our worship we are united with the Communion of Saints and with the whole company of heaven who serve the building of the Kingdom by their unceasing worship before the throne.

One day, the prophet Isaiah was at worship in the Temple in Jerusalem and had a vision of heaven (Isaiah 6). He was caught up into the angelic worship of God's holiness. This encounter vividly revealed to him the sinful reality of his own life and of the life of God's people and he desired to be changed. His guilt was swept away by the mercy of God. This is how his call to service arose. In the vision he then heard God's call for a messenger. 'Here am I; send me!'

In the year that King Uzziah died, I saw the LORD sitting on a throne, high and lofty; and the hem of his robe filled the temple. Seraphs were in attendance above him; each had six wings: with two they covered their faces, and with two they covered their feet, and with two they flew. And one called to another and said:

> *'Holy, holy, holy is the LORD of hosts;*
> *the whole earth is full of his glory.'*

The pivots on the thresholds shook at the voices of those who called, and the house filled with smoke. And I said: 'Woe is me! I am lost, for I am a man of unclean lips, and I live among a people of unclean lips; yet my eyes have seen the King, the LORD of hosts!'

Then one of the seraphs flew to me, holding a live coal that had been taken from the altar with a pair of tongs. The seraph touched my mouth with it and said: 'Now that this has touched your lips, your guilt has departed and your sin is blotted out.' Then I heard the voice of the LORD saying, 'Whom shall I send, and who will go for us? And I said, 'Here am I; send me!'

Isaiah 6.1–8

Christians can be accused of being so heavenly minded that they are of no earthly use. Unless we are heavenly minded, with worship and prayer as our mainspring, we shall definitely not be of any use at all. It is never a waste to linger in devotion because our adoration and thanksgiving are the very paths used by the Spirit of God to bring to birth in us that whole self which then does not fear being given away for the sake of others. St Augustine tells us that in the Eucharist we become what we eat, the Body of Christ. Then we, too, shall be blessed and broken and given out.

We have been called through that same Christ who, at supper with his disciples the night before he died, left the table, took off his outer robe and wrapped a towel around him. He then proceeded to wash his disciples' feet. Peter resisted, outraged that his master should behave towards him as a servant. But Jesus is enacting his most powerful parable. This kind of Messiah has come to save the whole world and these particular friends: a servant who takes to himself the weariness, the loss and the commitment to mistaken and wilful paths which these feet represent. He who is the Way, the Truth and the Life puts the lost on the right path, opens their minds to the truth and wonder of God's love and fills their emptiness with the life which knows no end. Jesus enacts for his friends a sacramental sign of the perfect attentiveness of God. The touch, indeed the caress of God offered to our battered feet, reveals the love which also disturbs us into service. Christians do not always have to be loud in their proclamation of the gospel, but their service must be eloquent in the language of this love.

On that night, Jesus gave his friends the gift of his lingering touch in this washing. He did not know exactly what the next hours might bring, other than that the crisis point in his ministry would be reached. He knew them intimately. He knew their fear, and could probably smell it on them. They would run away, even Peter. Some of the women alone would remain. Yet these actions express his confidence that God would go on using these women and men and their testimony of him, regardless of their weakness and fear. They did not understand then, he knew, but later they would begin to work it out together.

It is this confidence which comes through so strongly in Jesus' farewell discourses as presented by the writer of John's Gospel in chapters 14 to 17. They are troubled now and will go through all kinds of trials; but the Holy Spirit will come as their Comforter and Advocate. He tells them that they are no longer servants, but his friends so long as they do what he has commanded them. They are empowered not in their own strength but in his choosing them. So, he says, 'I appointed you to go and bear fruit, fruit that will last' (15.16). They must love one another as Christ has loved them. Yet Christ's concern is not just or even primarily for his immediate friends. His great priestly prayer in John 17 is not only for them:

> I ask not only on behalf of these, but also on behalf of those who will believe in me through their word.
>
> John 17.20

On a beach by the Sea of Galilee, the risen Christ completely restores Peter after his denials. The proof of love between them is that Peter will feed Christ's sheep and so serve the Shepherd who has already laid down his life for them.

The image of the shepherd is a familiar one for those who are considering a call to ministry, especially to the diaconate and priesthood. As we reflect on this image we might like to remember that it is normal for a shepherd courageously to protect the flock, but to do so in order to make a living out of them and to be realistic about losses. The shepherd who is our model has determined that the sheep should find their life in him. With what seems a reckless love to the prudent, this shepherd leaves the ninety-nine sheep to search for the one lost or wayward sheep. We live with the likelihood that we have been or might be that sheep, even as we are being shaped by the Spirit for service.

Mission impossible?

We have already reflected upon the extraordinary faith of Abraham and Sarah. They accept God's call to leave home at an age when they might have expected to put their feet up by the fire and live on their memories not in the hope of fresh experience. They are childless, yet they accept God's promise that their union will bring to birth a people more numerous than the sands of the seashore. Their faith and confidence in what appears impossible is mirrored in the experience of Zechariah and Elizabeth as they receive, dumbstruck, the news of the conception of John the Baptist.

Those who are going to be servants of others are not people who live a fantasy about a God who is wilfully going to interrupt the workings of creation on some whim. Servants are deeply realistic and earthy people. The point is rather that it is a realistic view of the world to see that extraordinary and miraculous things happen when people act with faith, courage and love.

Prophets like Isaiah and Amos find their prophetic voice when they begin to speak out against the practice of injustice. Concern about proper weights and measures and the practical care of foreigners and refugees are the litmus test of the health of the whole community and real commitment to God's covenant. As we believe in a God who has come to us that all people might have life and live it to the full, we also believe that we can change the world. There is nothing finally to fear: God has overcome all.

The more one thinks about it the more risky the incarnation seems. An unmarried girl from a backwater in the Roman Empire is chosen to be the mother of God. As St Bernard of Clairvaux says, the whole of creation held its breath waiting for Mary's 'Yes' to God.[1] Yet only his courage and conscience being fuelled by his dreaming of an angel achieve the co-operation of her bemused and conventional betrothed, Joseph. From this point he is transformed from the kindly man who is keen to save a scandal, to the indomitable parent who gives up all he has and becomes a refugee to save this boy who becomes his son. Even after that resolution in Joseph's mind and heart, the risk of infant mortality was part of God's emphatic self-giving. After the

fact of the incarnation itself, perhaps the most extraordinary part of the story is God's waiting on this woman. The
language of her being prepared by grace even before her
birth is an explanation of how this woman came to be so at
home in herself as a human being in love with God that she
could become the home of God. This is a revolutionary
development in the partnership which God seeks with
human beings in the reconciliation of all things earthly and
heavenly.

*In the sixth month the angel Gabriel was sent by God to a town in
Galilee called Nazareth, to a virgin engaged to a man whose name
was Joseph, of the house of David. The virgin's name was Mary. And
he came to her and said, 'Greetings, favoured one! The Lord is with
you.' But she was much perplexed by his words and pondered what
sort of greeting this might be. The angel said to her, 'Do not be
afraid, Mary, for you have found favour with God. And now, you will
conceive in your womb and bear a son, and you will name him Jesus.
He will be great, and will be called the Son of the Most High, and
the Lord God will give to him the throne of his ancestor David. He
will reign over the house of Jacob for ever, and of his kingdom there
will be no end.' Mary said to the angel, 'How can this be, since I am
a virgin?' The angel said to her, 'The Holy Spirit will come upon
you, and the power of the Most High will overshadow you; therefore
the child to be born will be holy; he will be called Son of God. And
now, your relative Elizabeth in her old age has also conceived a son;
and this is the sixth month for her who was said to be barren. For
nothing will be impossible with God.' Then Mary said, 'Here am I,
the servant of the Lord; let it be with me according to your word.'
Then the angel departed from her.*

Luke 1.26–38

Mary sees her heavily pregnant previously barren
cousin, Elizabeth, and her heart sings with joy and passion
about how the world has been changed for ever, and she

finds the words out of reflection on the prayer of Hannah, her forebear in faith and the courageous mother of another decisive child, the prophet Samuel. Through her, God was making the divine glory concrete, making hope real and the value of the poor the gold standard of the Kingdom. In popular religious thinking when Luke's Gospel was being written, sin had come into the world because sexually rapacious women had fallen for bad angels and had brought evil to birth. Women were to wear shawls and hats because they were especially vulnerable to angelic invasion through their heads. In Luke's account of the annunciation an angel comes not with assault in mind but to bear God's promise of the ultimate gift of love. He is met by a virgin who makes a free and adult choice. Like any of us who are chosen, Mary does not have perfect understanding. She offers herself in trust and not fear as a free child of God on behalf of so many who are beyond the direct orbit of her choice.

It is a sign of the same revolution that women, in a society which gave no value to their testimony in court, should be the first witnesses of the resurrection, since theirs, with Mary, were the faces of love which Jesus could see from the cross. It is they who are told to tell the other disciples to seek the risen Christ in Galilee. Already they are being led back on to the road aiming to keep track with the people and places which Christ has already claimed.

The bonds of love to set others free

Chapters 18 and 20 of the Prophecy of Jeremiah mark a new departure in the history and literature of the Bible. For the first time we see the record of the deep feelings of an individual – the prophet himself. He curses the day he was born, life is so intolerable. The reason is that he is re-proached, derided and his very life is endangered because he speaks God's word, speaking out against injustice and false religion. The only path to a safe life is to remain quiet, but this is not an option:

> *If I say, 'I will not mention him, or speak any more in his name', then within me there is something like a burning fire shut up in my bones; I am weary with holding it in, and I cannot.*
>
> Jeremiah 20.9

Being a faithful witness no matter the cost is key to any sense of calling for others and is a characteristic of servants of God down the ages. On 5 November we see Catherine wheels light up the sky along with other fireworks. The wheel takes its name from the martyrdom of St Catherine of Alexandria in the early fourth century, who was broken on a wheel not only for refusing to marry an emperor who was not a Christian but for refuting the arguments of a posse of pagan philosophers. In an earlier persecution a century before, Polycarp, Bishop of Smyrna, was arrested after serving forty years as bishop. He was given the option to save his life by renouncing his faith. He said: 'I have been Christ's servant for 86 years and he has done me no harm. Can I now blaspheme my King and my Saviour?' He was promptly burned at the stake.

Closer to our own time, Maximilian Kolbe was a Polish Franciscan friar who continued to publish Christian newspapers after the Nazi invasion of his country in 1939 that bravely condemned the horror of the occupation. He was sent to Auschwitz in 1941. Against the odds, he continued to celebrate mass in the camp. When several prisoners were selected for death as retribution for an escape, Kolbe volunteered to take the place of one of the condemned men.

Such clear correspondence between word and action, however costly in our own lives, is what we are all called to pray will be evident in our paths as servants of the truth.

This does not suggest that our service of others means that we should deliberately seek trouble, or even martyrdom. The seeking of martyrdom by Christian zealots in the early Church was regularly condemned. What matters is that we pray for the grace to be the small person who rises to fight for a greater cause if the need arises.

Oscar Romero

A retiring and quiet scholarly pastor in El Salvador in Latin America, Oscar Romero appeared in a violent and deeply divided country to be the choice as an archbishop who would not cause trouble to the corrupt elite and their death squads. He rapidly understood, however, that his office demanded that he give a voice to the poor and downtrodden. He was warned to be quiet, but gently persisted. He was shot dead at the altar by an unknown gunman in 1980.

The Gospels record that Jesus himself attested that the greatest of those who could not keep silent was John the Baptist, the great forerunner. His uncompromising preaching of repentance drew crowds into the wilderness of Judea. Jesus says to the people about John:

> *What did you go out into the wilderness to look at? A reed shaken by the wind? What then did you go out to see? . . . A prophet? Yes, I tell you, and more than a prophet. This is the one about whom it is written,*
>
> > *'See, I am sending my messenger ahead of you,*
> > *who will prepare your way before you.'*
>
> *I tell you, among those born of women no one is greater than John; yet the least in the kingdom of God is greater than he.*
>
> Luke 7.24–8

John's message favoured no one because of their perceived authority – soldiers, senior clergy, influential tax officials, even Herod the ruler were all under the same judgement. This service of the truth cost him his freedom and his life.

Anyone, of course, can fulminate against one kind of injustice but can actually either be in the service of a replacement variety, or be exploiting the platform of criticism to establish power for themselves under the banner of protest.

John's way is not a perverse and costly means for the servant to gain power or a reputation. This is the way to point away from himself to Christ. Twice in John chapter 1 the Baptist points to Jesus and announces that he is the Lamb of God. On the second occasion he tells his own disciples, aware, no doubt, that they would leave him to seek out this Jesus. This is precisely what John sought: he is the bridegroom's friend who is now overjoyed to hear the bridegroom's voice. 'For this reason my joy has been fulfilled. He must increase, but I must decrease' (John 3.29b–30). The best service of any servant is to point others to the Lamb. The only way to enact the costly service of the truth about God and about the human beings we are made to become is to model it on the service of Christ himself. He is the Lamb who sacrificed himself on the cross that we all might live, and who accepted the bonds of love that all people might be free and flourish.

John and so many others have been eloquent examples to us of the risks taken by the messenger, not least the risk of death. Most of the people who die as martyrs do not become servants of Christ in the world in expectation of a martyr's death. After all, the first martyr, Stephen, started out by being called to be a diplomatic provisions manager. It could happen to any of us, but the reality is that most of us will not face that direct danger.

This is not to say that there are no other costs for us to be aware of and which we may have to embrace. Accepting a calling for others will inevitably risk a dramatic change in our circumstances. Take Ruth the Moabite's decision to follow her mother-in-law Naomi: it changed the rest of her life. She goes into the unknown for love. Her steadfastness transforms Naomi's grief at the loss of all her family and she eventually renews hope for the future by sharing her child. She is also the stranger in a foreign land who goes first to the margins, gleaning left-over grain.

> *Where you go, I will go; where you lodge, I will lodge; your people shall be my people, and your God my God.*
>
> Ruth 1.16

During the centuries following the conversion of Ireland, countless Irish monks and missionaries travelled across the known world and beyond its bounds to carry the message of salvation. The Irish, great lovers of home, invented a new category of martyrdom which was to leave behind the safety of what is known and cherished to venture out into the margins. It was monks like these who were converting northern Britain even as Augustine was arriving on the shores of Kent. It was these women and men who carried with them a joy in God which celebrated the beauty of creation and the flourishing of all things. It is this kind of martyrdom which we may embrace to some degree if we genuinely give ourselves away. Giving up what we know and embracing an as yet unknown future can be terrifying. Yet the Irish monks kept going because they knew God was already there ahead of them waiting to be revealed in unexpected places and people. Like them, we are called to those margins to reveal them as the centre of God's activity. Along the way, we shall be changed both by the travelling and the arriving. Like Ruth, we do not just accompany others, but find our own true home.

You must be mad!

Any personality profile of the prophets does not suggest
that they would find selection for ministries within the
Church either satisfying or successful. Isaiah went around
Jerusalem naked for three years to make a point. Both he
and Hosea burdened their poor children with dreadful
names with meanings like 'Hastening for Plunder' to
underline a point of prophecy. The way in which the
prophet Ezekiel seeks to embody the plight of the exiles in
Babylon borders on the pathological. None of this is
surprising: the prophetic tradition in Israel is ecstatic and
very strange to most of us. One of the good things about
Martin Scorcese's *The Last Temptation of Christ* is the way in
which the film represents that tradition surviving into the
late-flowering of prophecy in John the Baptist and his disciples.

We know from the Gospel accounts that the people who
first recognized Jesus for who he truly was were the so-
called 'mad' people. It is no wonder that all we really know
about Mary Magdalene without speculative leaps is that she
was cured of seven devils. Her relationship with Christ and
her calling to be a disciple and witness are all tied up with
her being freed from madness and the dreadful loneliness
and risk of abuse that goes with it. As an important woman
and as a personality under threat, Mary is a doubly danger-
ous model for discipleship. It is right that she be so and that
we should resist the attempts late in the tradition of literary
and artistic interpretation to undermine her role with male
projections about the reformed prostitute.

The most remarkable representation of Mary in art is the
wood and gilt statue of her in old age by Donatello. The
fifteenth-century sculptor, himself an old man, pays Mary
the greatest favour in depicting her as a real woman
stretched to the limit by the long path she had chosen of
asceticism and penitence. The dominant theme of the cult

which developed around her alleged burial place at Vézelay was of the saint who chose to give her life after the resurrection to the hidden life of prayer, reparation and ascetic denial in a cave.

This tradition thus represented in the sculpture is illuminating at more than one level. In later life Donatello sculpted statues of both Mary Magdalene and John the Baptist. Both are studies made in old age but also each figure reveals a person living with great inner tension. The boundary between prophetic insight and popular conceptions of madness maybe is not wide. Both characters operate with at least one layer of skin less than most people. They are acutely conscious that the pattern of their lives makes them outsiders, and yet being on the outside is the key to being such significant servants of the one who was crucified outside the gate among thieves.

Perhaps Mary is such a good servant not only because she can minister to all kinds of outsiders since she has been mentally ill in the past but because she still lives with its consequences. When Jesus healed lepers they did not grow their limbs back. The experience of many people living with mental illness is that a key breakthrough is to be treated as a whole person and not as a walking diagnosis. Jesus saw Mary as that person.

One of the most risky ventures for a person who hears voices, and faces terrors rising from within, is to be in silence and alone. The image of Mary as an ascetic hermit living alone, who maybe still hears voices but only listens for the one, still, small voice of God, would be a powerful sign of what transformation God can work in each of us. In redeeming our situation and our personality, God makes each of us signs of transformation for others.

The image also serves to counter any illusion we may have that our calling will assuredly be functionally useful. After being part of the momentous events of Christ's ministry, his crucifixion and resurrection, retreating to a cave does not appear at first sight to be a world-changing choice. An interesting feature of the restoration of the Donatello sculpture in the 1960s, however, is that the original paint on the statue revealed this old woman still with streaks of gold in her hair. There is still glory about her, not her own glory but the glory of the one whom she loves and through whom she prays for the flourishing of the world. This is where all service begins, continues and ends. There is no qualitative distinction between the contemplative and the active servant: all is rooted in the adoration of God.

Divine choreography

Sydney Carter's hymn, *The Lord of the Dance*, finds a modern form for the medieval Easter carols which proclaimed the good news of the resurrection in dance as well as song. A published sermon[2] of the late Michael Stancliffe refers to the whole life of Christ as a dance in step both with the love of the Father and with the life of human beings. This was the life which triumphantly danced through death into new creation. Those who really caught the rhythm danced with a kind of clod-hopping enthusiasm. This dance jolted to a halt at the crucifixion but they were amazed to discover that the Lord appeared to partner them again. It was the joy of the apostles and disciples to dance through the rest of their lives, bringing others to learn the steps and to interpret the movement. Before many people had the will to dance, Jesus had to show them the joy of reconciliation.

The Gospels (especially that of Luke) again and again show us Jesus at parties with unlikely mixtures of guests, some of them definitely uninvited. We may suppose that people went away from these parties with a new lightness of step because they had been forgiven. No wonder they could join in the dance. They were tax-collectors, shepherds, fishermen, prostitutes, soldiers, priests, teachers.

They were all people offered a fresh understanding of
themselves in a new relationship to God and with people
whom they would never have expected to know. Michael
Stancliffe is clear that the service of the dance bears no relation to the 'grim groove of moral duty'.[3] You can usually
tell where such people have been by the unwelcome effect
evident on those whom they have sought to serve. What
really marks the infinite variety of people right up to today
who are harbingers of glory and love is that they become
servants of reconciliation and attentive teachers of the
dance.

Some questions

1 What are the starting points for a calling to serve others
   as a Christian?
2 Who are your models of service – in the Bible, in
   Christian history and among people you know?
3 How do you allow other people to serve Christ in you?

CHAPTER 4

The Call of Jesus

Kevin Scully

God's love is always creative. Out of love Jesus Christ is called. His life is an outworking of that love, but what do we mean when we claim he was called by God? His entire existence was lived out responsively to that call, but how and why he did so is open to interpretation. The writers of the New Testament attempt to respond to the questions raised by his ministry – just as each individual disciple must.

A questioning call

'Is it me?' These are the first words uttered by Jesus in Dennis Potter's play *Son of Man*. For some people the idea that Jesus would, or even need to, ask such a question is shocking. But then the Christian faith contains one of the greatest possible shocks: God became one of us. The opening question of Potter's play echoes one of the fundamental ideas of Christianity. The fully human Jesus, while fully God, grew as a person and in knowledge of the world. Perhaps knowledge of himself came with that growth. This is based on an earlier premise which is called creation. Just as all things were called out of the Godhead and developed, God could be seen to call himself from among humanity. This was Jesus, who developed and grew in God's image.

This can lead to some puzzling questions. If God is all powerful, then why was it necessary that the frailty of a human form was required? And, as Judas Iscariot asks in the musical *Jesus Christ Superstar*, why did God choose such a backward time in such a strange land to do it? Why did Jesus call such a strange assortment of followers? Why did he provoke the various authorities of his time which led to a confrontation that ended with his death?

These questions can be heard in just about any forum: a pub, a study group, a bus, a tutorial at university, over coffee, in school. The questions have been raised before. Indeed, for some people the Gospels of Matthew, Mark, Luke and John are attempts to pose, puzzle over and answer some of these questions. Not surprisingly, they come at the issues from different angles.

Any study of the Gospels makes us realize there are similarities and differences in these accounts of the life of Jesus. Sometimes stories get tangled up. Some incidents appear in only one of the Gospels; others are similar, but with some differing details and emphases. There are passages that appear in some, but not in all of the accounts. The different writers are assumed to be addressing different people. And this means they have distinct things to say. Taking a snapshot of the four Gospels, as we are about to do, can add to the confusion but it is enlightening to see how differently they understood Jesus' call.

A Jesus for the Jews: Matthew

The Gospel of Matthew has been described as the most Jewish and anti-Jewish of the biblical accounts of Jesus. There are many references to the writings of what Christians call the Old Testament. The writer points to oracles, traditions and history, and tries to show how they have come true or reached fulfilment in what Jesus said or did. Great store is placed on genealogy, with its hiccups in the line because of foreigners and outsiders, especially among the women, which has its end point in Joseph, 'the husband of Mary, of whom Jesus was born, who is called the Messiah' (Matt. 1.16). In this way Jesus is shown to be the long-expected deliverer of the nation of Israel. The teachings of Jesus are brought together in a lengthy series of sayings, often referred to as the Sermon on the Mount. Much is also made of Jesus' teaching on the Kingdom, the overthrow and replacement of Roman domination. One unanswered question remains for Matthew: if Jesus is the one they have been waiting for, why do not Jewish people acclaim him as the Messiah?

A suffering Jesus: Mark

> *The beginning of the good news of Jesus Christ, the Son of God.*
> Mark 1.1

The Gospel of Mark pulls no punches. The style is direct from its very opening. There are no references to genealogy, nor mention of Jesus' birth. It is an adult Jesus who makes his way to the Jordan to be baptized by John, an event which leads to what might be seen as his call: 'And just as he was coming up out of the water, he saw the heavens torn apart and the Spirit descending like a dove on him. And a voice came from heaven, "You are my Son, the Beloved; with you I am well pleased"' (Mark 1.10–11). Plenty of action follows. There are accounts of what he did, including many journeys on which people followed him, and what he said. The Gospel moves quickly through the last days of Jesus, the passion of Mark being the briefest and perhaps most brutal. There is also a puzzle about the conclusion of the Gospel, with alternative endings. It is a useful exercise to read parts of the Bible as if it were any other book, say a thriller. It is especially effective to read Mark this way.

A Jesus for his followers: Luke

Luke's Gospel is the most detailed of what are known as the Synoptic Gospels, Matthew, Mark and Luke. There are many aspects of it which set it apart from its companions: it has the longest narratives of the birth of Jesus, including much of the familiar Christmas story; its early parts include poems and songs, three of which have become great hymns of the Church – the Benedictus, Magnificat and Nunc Dimittis. Luke is the most concerned with the mind of Jesus and what thought lay behind his actions. Because of that, his teaching to his followers takes on a deeper resonance. The grace of God is revealed in Jesus and the most unlikely candidates – sinners and tax-collectors – reap the benefits. People change because of their encounters with Jesus and, at the end of the Gospel, his followers are told to wait for a special blessing:

> And see, I am sending upon you what my Father promised; so stay here in the city until you have been clothed with power from on high.
>
> Luke 24.49

The account of that clothing – Pentecost and the founding of the Church – is told in the Book of Acts, written by the author of Luke.

Jesus the Word: John

It is clear from the opening sentences of the Gospel of John that this account is different from the Synoptics. It is generally thought to have been written after and perhaps apart from the Synoptic Gospels. In John the word, what is said, is of the utmost importance because Jesus is the

Word, the human expression of God. Much of what Jesus has to say, and where he says it, contrasts with the other Gospels: he uses long speeches, with sentences that often have an inversion of meaning within them; there are virtually no parables; and most of the events, many unique to John, take place in Jerusalem at or near festival times. He makes clear that he is the Son of God and it is this more than anything which leads him to being seen as a blasphemer by the authorities. John repeatedly calls the opponents or doubters of Jesus 'the Jews'. It is in this Gospel that all the 'I am' sayings are recorded: the bread of life, the light of the world, the door for the sheep, the good shepherd, the resurrection and the life, the way, the truth and the life, the true vine.

The call of the Gospels

Christians are often told they need to be Christ-like. This can be confusing because no ordinary human can be God. What they are being urged to do is to attempt to make their lives a mirror of the life of Jesus. That involves trying to echo the actions of Jesus and will also mean trying to interpret what prompted Jesus to take the actions he did.

The call to challenge and revolution

Then Levi gave a great banquet for him in his house; and there was a large crowd of tax-collectors and others sitting at the table with them. The Pharisees and their scribes were complaining to his disciples, saying, 'Why do you eat and drink with tax-collectors and sinners?' Jesus answered, 'Those who are well have no need of a physician, but those who are sick; I have come to call not the righteous but sinners to repentance.'

Luke 5.29–32

Throughout the Gospels we see the ways in which Jesus responds to his call as the Son of God. Jesus broke the boundaries of the Jewish Law and the social expectations of his time. He allowed women to mix with him and they often spoke to him directly, asking him for favours and teaching. He touched and was touched by those who were considered unclean and, by allowing that to happen, would have been made unclean himself.

His actions break more than the barriers of social acceptability. They are provocative. In the Gospels of Luke and John, Jesus either encounters personally, or tells a story which features, the good actions and motivations of a despised people, the Samaritans. He often speaks of inward marks of cleanliness rather than external signs, and he outrages bystanders by telling people their sins are forgiven.

When he is confronted with these breaches in the religious and social codes, Jesus often responds provocatively. On a number of occasions he is accused of breaking the Sabbath by healing on the Jewish holy day, but he does not apologize. Rather, he questions those who would convict others of a religious crime. In this way Jesus repeatedly challenges the motives of those who are being formed up against him, as well as the social structures which inform their thinking. He underlines that a new order is beginning.

Time and again Jesus takes the contrary view to the one that could be expected, and this is not confined to his critics. He does not protect his own followers from his challenge. He tells them to look to their own lives. He rebukes them for timidity and stupidity. He challenges them to dare to see their own circumstances recast, revolutionized into the Kingdom of God which, at one point he tells them, is actually among them. He tells the rich to give away what they have. He tells children they have a special place. He says wisdom is given to the simple. Jesus sees what those around him do not see: the vision of the blind, the athleticism of the paralysed, the forgiveness of sinners, the life in the dead.

In his final days Jesus gives some of the clearest indications that the call on him is the call he makes to those who want to follow him. He washes the feet of his disciples, telling them to go and do the same. He takes bread and wine, saying that they convey life (his body and blood) and commands them to do this in his memory.

The repeated confrontations and subversion of social and political norms are pivotal in the events which lead to his being seized, tried and killed. And with that comes one of the most revolutionary acts of the Christian faith: the triumph over death in the resurrection.

The call to healing and repentance

The scribes and Pharisees brought a woman who had been caught in adultery; and making her stand before all of them, they said to him, 'Teacher, this woman was caught in the very act of committing adultery. Now in the law Moses commanded us to stone such women. Now what do you say?' They said this to test him, so that they might have some charge to bring against him. Jesus bent down and wrote with his finger on the ground. When they kept on questioning him, he straightened up and said to them, 'Let anyone among you who is without sin be the first to throw a stone at her.' And once again he bent down and wrote on the ground. When they heard it, they went away one by one, beginning with the elders; and Jesus was left alone with the woman standing before him. Jesus straightened up and said to her, 'Woman, where are they? Has no one condemned you?' She said, 'No one, sir.' And Jesus said, 'Neither do I condemn you. Go your way, and from now on do not sin again.'

John 8.3–11

To concentrate on the physical results in the stories of cures in the Gospels runs the risk of restricting their power. The healing power of Jesus goes far beyond the physical. Healing is about restoring the whole person: body, mind and spirit. In many of his encounters, Jesus first tells the ones to whom he restores lost powers that they are forgiven. In some of the exchanges he has with those who witness the healings it is his pronouncement of sins forgiven that causes outrage. They are sometimes happy to see someone restored to physical health, but to say this mirrors an inner healing, a spiritual making whole, is too much for his critics.

As he walked along, he saw a man blind from birth. His disciples asked him, 'Rabbi, who sinned, this man or his parents, that he was born blind?' Jesus answered, 'Neither this man nor his parents sinned; he was born blind so that God's works might be revealed in him. We must work the works of him who sent me while it is day; night is coming when no one can work. As long as I am in the world, I am the light of the world.' When he had said this, he spat on the ground and made mud with the saliva and spread the mud on the man's eyes, saying to him, 'Go, wash in the pool of Siloam' (which means Sent). Then he went and washed and came back able to see. The neighbours and those who had seen him before as a beggar began to ask, 'Is this not the man who used to sit and beg?' Some were saying, 'It is he.' Others were saying, 'No, but it is someone like him.' He kept saying, 'I am the man.' But they kept asking him, 'Then how were your eyes opened?' He answered, 'The man called Jesus made mud, spread it on my eyes, and said to me, "Go to Siloam and wash." Then I went and washed and received my sight.' They said to him, 'Where is he?' He said, 'I do not know.'

They brought to the Pharisees the man who had formerly been blind. Now it was a sabbath day when Jesus made the mud and opened his eyes. Then the Pharisees also began to ask him how he had received his sight. He said to them, 'He put mud on my eyes. Then I washed, and now I see.' Some of the Pharisees said, 'This man is not from God, for he does not observe the sabbath.' But others said,

'How can a man who is a sinner perform such signs?' And they were divided. So they said again to the blind man, 'What do you say about him? It was your eyes he opened.' He said, 'He is a prophet.'

The Jews did not believe that he had been blind and had received his sight until they called the parents of the man who had received his sight and asked them, 'Is this your son, who you say was born blind? How then does he now see?' His parents answered, 'We know that this is our son, and that he was born blind; but we do not know how it is that now he sees, nor do we know who opened his eyes. Ask him; he is of age. He will speak for himself.' His parents said this because they were afraid of the Jews; for the Jews had already agreed that anyone who confessed Jesus to be the Messiah would be put out of the synagogue. Therefore his parents said, 'He is of age; ask him.'

So for the second time they called the man who had been blind, and they said to him, 'Give glory to God! We know that this man is a sinner.' He answered, 'I do not know whether he is a sinner. One thing I do know, that though I was blind, now I see.' They said to him, 'What did he do to you? How did he open your eyes?' He answered them, 'I have told you already, and you would not listen. Why do you want to hear it again? Do you also want to become his disciples?' Then they reviled him, saying, 'You are his disciple, but we are disciples of Moses. We know that God has spoken to Moses, but as for this man, we do not know where he comes from.' The man answered, 'Here is an astonishing thing! You do not know where he comes from, and yet he opened my eyes. We know that God does not listen to sinners, but he does listen to one who worships him and obeys his will. Never since the world began has it been heard that anyone opened the eyes of a person born blind. If this man were not from God, he could do nothing.' They answered him, 'You were born entirely in sins, and are you trying to teach us?' And they drove him out.

John 9.1–34

One good example of this is in the story of the blind man (above) who receives his sight in the Gospel of John. The account starts with a discussion on sin. Is it the man himself or his parents who sinned? Jesus responds obliquely: the

work of God will be revealed through him. Sight is given to
the man but those who witness are not satisfied; they still
need someone to blame. They accuse Jesus of being a
sinner. Another discussion about the nature of God and
those who do his will follows. They accuse Jesus again. Jesus
is asking them to look to themselves. This is part of the
challenging and revolutionary call of Jesus. But it can lead
to wholeness beyond the immediate beneficiary. It can heal
societies. Those confronting Jesus take it amiss, thinking
they are being accused of blindness:

> Jesus said to them, 'If you were blind, you would not have sin. But
> now that you say, "We see", your sin remains.'
>
> John 9.41

This can also be seen when spiritual, rather than physical,
disability is being dealt with. In the confrontation with the
woman taken in adultery, Jesus is more concerned with her
accusers. In a similar way his followers are urged to look at
their own motives before entering into judgement upon
others. He tells them to remove the log from their own eye
before attempting to remove the speck from a neighbour's
(Matt. 7.4–5) and advises them to pluck out an eye if it leads
to sin. This, then, is about honesty in self-examination.

Yet it is mistaken to imagine such examination of
motives is confined to personal issues. Systems and societies are in need of questioning and confrontation.
Communities, businesses, societies and churches can and
have fallen short of this gospel imperative. Content to the
edge of complacency, they can forget the fundamentals and
begin to ignore, sideline and oppress others. An examination of what groups believe should be compared with how
they operate. That way social healing lies. Where motives
are analysed and we are found lacking, changes can, should

and sometimes do follow. This is living up to the gospel challenge to repent and, by repenting, to allow healing.

The call to wilderness and prayer

And whenever you pray, do not be like the hypocrites; for they love to stand and pray in the synagogues and at the street corners, so that they may be seen by others. Truly I tell you, they have received their reward. But whenever you pray, go into your room and shut the door and pray to your Father who is in secret; and your Father who sees in secret will reward you. When you are praying, do not heap up empty phrases as the Gentiles do; for they think they will be heard because of their many words. Do not be like them, for your Father knows what you need before you ask him.

Matthew 6.5–8

An important aspect of the life of Jesus is prayer. There are a number of beguiling references to Jesus going to a remote place to pray. He is not always successful, and often the crowds find him and he is forced to move on.

A number of key moments in the Gospels come when Jesus has removed himself from the round of teaching, healing and even companionship. One is the transfiguration. After a series of miracles, confrontations and healings, Jesus goes to a remote place, a mountain. He is not with a crowd, but a small group. Peter, James and John see Jesus transfigured in the company of the great prophets Moses and Elijah.

A darker incident is reported to have taken place away from others. In Matthew's Gospel, after having received the baptism of John the Baptist, Jesus goes into the wilderness and there undergoes a series of temptations. In a mysterious description, Jesus and the devil test each other with the things of the world and spirit, with scripture quoted for good measure. This all occurs while Jesus is 'famished' after having fasted for forty days and nights.

Another key moment is the prayer of Jesus before his arrest and passion. Again he has removed himself from his disciples, once more with those who had seen him transfigured, when he prays for the possibility of his not having to undergo the trials before him. His prayer is, however, not for himself but that the will of God be done.

It would be tempting to concentrate only on the occasions of Jesus' praying alone, or when removed from larger groups, but to do so runs the risk of an unbalanced view of the prayer life of Jesus. He is often reported praying before and after his healing miracles. He attends synagogues, as was his custom, the Gospels report. He engages in traditional prayers at the Last Supper and then institutes the holy meal that has become the touchstone of the Christian faith.

Every follower of Jesus is called to pray. We pray alone, as advised by Jesus, and pray together. We do so in groups which can be informal and within set liturgies. But in everything, like those who heard Jesus teach, we should follow the pattern of Jesus. It was after he himself had been praying that he gave his teaching on prayer:

When you pray, say:

Father, hallowed be your name.
Your kingdom come.
Give us each day our daily bread.
And forgive us our sins,
for we ourselves forgive everyone indebted to us.
And do not bring us to the time of trial.
Luke 11.2–4

The call to service and suffering

> So Jesus called them and said to them, 'You know that among the Gentiles those whom they recognize as their rulers lord it over them, and their great ones are tyrants over them. But it is not so among you; but whoever wishes to become great among you must be your servant, and whoever wishes to be first among you must be the slave of all. For the Son of Man came not to be served but to serve, and to give his life as a ransom for many.'
>
> Mark 10.42–5

Jesus was direct and often uncompromising in his relationships with others. This was sometimes experienced as provocative or subversive; at other times he was single-minded and transparent. Straightforward responses to a human need for healing or explanation often resulted in what appeared to be a threat to the established order. Such openness to others' needs is captured in the simple question Jesus posed to those who came to him: 'What do you want me to do for you?' Some wanted to see, others to walk, others to be free from some crippling disease. Others asked not for themselves but on behalf of loved ones. We have already seen how Jesus would add to the significance of the request by saying that sins had been forgiven.

When Jesus was teaching those who would follow him, he repeatedly urged that they should be of use to others. Service is not an added extra but of the essence in taking up the call to follow him. After the parable of the Good Samaritan, which contrasts the behaviour of those who might be expected to assist a man – a priest and a Levite – it is the outsider, the Samaritan, who acts charitably. After his actions have been praised, Jesus is explicit: 'Go and do likewise' (Luke 10.37).

The parable is an illustration to the disciples after Jesus has sent them out as 'labourers into his harvest' (Luke 10.2). At the Last Supper he shows his disciples how they are to follow him. He takes the job of a servant. He washes their feet. And he ensures that the disciples have not missed the point.

> So if I, your Lord and Teacher, have washed your feet, you also ought to wash one another's feet. For I have set you an example, that you also should do as I have done to you.
>
> John 13.14–15

Jesus repeatedly tells his followers that their calling may be tough and unpopular. He tells them that families will be divided, worldly respect and esteem may diminish. He warns them to expect hostility and suffering. This again is a mirror of what he himself is to undergo. The very basis of Christian faith involves a dichotomy: the seeming failure of the cross is transfigured into a symbol of victory. Through the death of Jesus his followers can find freedom. Such an inversion is central to Jesus' teaching: you lose your life to save it; by becoming small you can be great; by serving you can lead.

These elements are captured in the first line of Dennis Potter's play. Jesus asks a question about his own mission to the world: 'Is it me?' Likewise, anyone who wants to think seriously about the Christian vocation can expect a similar question: 'Is it you?'

Some questions

1 What are the fundamental marks of Jesus' call to be the Son of God?

2 How could we change to make our lives more 'Christ-like'?
3 What forms of service are being required of you at work, at home and in the Church?

CHAPTER 5

The Call of Disciples

David Stephenson

This chapter will focus on the calling of the first followers of Jesus, both before and after his death, resurrection and ascension, and the giving of the Spirit at Pentecost. The aim is not simply historical; the manner in which the first followers of Jesus modelled his life and ministry gives us direction and inspiration in how we may also reflect his life and ministry.

The calling and ministry of Jesus were unique and special; and yet all Christian ministry finds its roots and identity here. From the beginning of his public ministry Jesus called men and women to follow him. This is the root meaning of 'disciple' – one who follows in the footsteps and after the example of their teacher. So, from the outset Jesus ministered in company with others whom he had called to share with him the proclamation and demonstration of the nearness of God's Kingdom. As disciples, those called by Jesus were expected to model their lives after the pattern of their master. In other words, disciples are called to be imitators of Christ.

> *For I have set you an example, that you also should do as I have done to you. Very truly, I tell you, servants are not greater than their master, nor are messengers greater than the one who sent them.*
>
> John 13.15–16

It is also tempting to see the calling and ministries of the earliest followers of Jesus as unique and special, particularly those who were called to be apostles. But their ministries (and all other particular ministries subsequently) were focused on enabling all the baptized to fulfil their calling to be imitators of Christ: 'The task of ministry is to serve the church, but to serve it by itself first living out the suffering redeeming life of Christ in the world, in order that the church as a whole may do likewise.'[1] At the heart of the calling of disciples is the challenge to reflect the life and ministry of Jesus.

Four key themes for our own calling will emerge from this examination of the calling of disciples in the New Testament period:

- Each person is called to reflect the life and ministry of Jesus in our own particular and unique ways, with our personal histories and personalities; and even with our limitations, weaknesses and failings.
- We are called to reflect the life and ministry of Jesus together.
- We are called to reflect the life and ministry of Jesus through an expanding of personal horizons.
- We are called to reflect the life and ministry of Jesus especially through an identification with the suffering and death of Jesus.

Jesus calls all kinds of disciples

Two things are immediately striking about those called by Jesus to be his disciples – their ordinariness and their diversity. None of the disciples seems to have had any formal qualifications or particular social status. From fishermen to tax-collectors to a woman of 'ill repute'; from rural labourers to the disreputable and suspect: Jesus did not choose members of an academic or wealthy or powerful elite to be the ambassadors of the reign of God.

So the first disciples were a rag-bag assortment of individuals, contrasting with each other in their convictions, lifestyles and personalities. The Gospels only give us hints of these contrasts in the varying responses of the disciples to Jesus, amid the disputes that arose between them and from what we know of their particular backgrounds.

Peter, a fisherman who immediately left the source of his livelihood to follow Jesus, remained impulsive and enthusiastic beyond his capacity to deliver on his promises. Peter was the first to confess Jesus as the Messiah, the Son of the living God, before immediately rejecting Jesus' own predictions of his impending suffering and death – revelation and insight giving way to lack of vision and nerve. Peter steps out of a boat to walk across the lake to Jesus only to be overcome by fear seconds later. At the Last Supper he vows to remain faithful to Jesus, even if it should cost his life; only hours later he denies even knowing Jesus. Thomas, by contrast, is known and loved for his cautious faith, seeking clarification even when Jesus suggests his teaching is obvious and refusing to believe that Jesus has risen from the dead unless he can see and touch Jesus for himself.

Among the twelve was Matthew, a tax-collector, and so a collaborator with the hated occupying Roman rulers; and Simon, the Zealot, a political revolutionary who would have been dedicated to the overthrow of the imperial government. There is no hint of dispute between them, but it does not take much imagination to infer some initial suspicion from such contrasting backgrounds.

Some of the disciples, like Peter, James and John, were willing to respond immediately to the call of Jesus; others showed more reluctance, speaking of the pull of family commitments. Some were expected and willing to leave everything to follow; others such as Mary, Martha and Lazarus remained in their homes and served Jesus there.

It would be wonderful to know more, to have fuller biographies of the first followers of Jesus. But at least we are given a taste of the rich variety that Jesus seems to have celebrated in his choosing of the twelve, and in his defence of some of his followers' lifestyles and customs to those eager to criticize and condemn. A mother of five in North East England, former lab-technician and actively exploring a vocation to the priesthood, might still doubt that she is the 'right sort of person' but she would not be out of place among those Jesus called his disciples and nor would the ex-Baptist drawn to Anglo-Catholicism but uncertain what it is all about; nor the young man who finds the *Star Wars* films a source of inspiration and theological insight!

Later in this chapter the theme of variety will be picked up again as we look at the diversity of gifts and ministries valued and celebrated within the early Church.

An awareness that we are called to reflect the life and ministry of Jesus in our own particular and unique ways according to our own personality will alert us to our weaknesses as well as our strengths. Each of us has our own particular personal histories, limitations and failings: how do these stand in relation to our calling? These issues have already been alluded to, but the example of the woman who anointed Jesus with ointment in the house of Simon the Pharisee (Luke 7.36–50) provides further illumination. Once again we are given no details of the woman's personal story: she is introduced to us simply as 'a woman in the city, who was a sinner' (v. 37). Although she clearly had some kind of past that made her unacceptable to Simon the Pharisee, Jesus openly receives her ministry of tenderness and devotion. In calling people Jesus does not seek to deny or cover up their past, but to change their relationship to it, so that it becomes a source of freedom and potentially useful in bearing witness to the upside-down Kingdom of God.

Jesus calls disciples to be together

As well as gathering a varied group of people to be his followers, Jesus also called them together. While continuing to cherish their diversity Jesus forms them into a group whose core identity is in doing the will of his 'Father in heaven': they are his 'brother and sister and mother' (Matt. 12.50).

For much of the Gospels the disciples are with Jesus, learning from his words and actions; but as his apprentices he also expects them to learn from their own experience of ministry. When he sends them out to minister in his name they go in pairs. Although this could be for their own safety, there are no instances where Jesus indicates he has solo ministry in mind for his followers. He always addresses them together – either the inner band of three (Peter, James and John), or the twelve or a wider group of disciples.

The theme of the essentially corporate nature of ministry in the New Testament will be picked up again later in this chapter, looking at the life and ministry of the early Church. Although it is not made explicit in the Gospels, the corporate nature of ministry in the early Church is seen as fundamental to reflecting the life of Jesus. This is especially clear in Paul's image of the Church with its many members being the Body of Christ.

Disciples are sent

Central to ideas of the call of the first disciples, especially the twelve, was that they were sent. This, in fact, is the root meaning of the word 'apostle'. In such a way too the disciples were called to reflect the life and ministry of Jesus: 'As the Father has sent me, so I send you' (John 20.21). They are his fully accredited agents.

Part of the meaning of being sent suggests leaving something behind and going on to something new. This could well

entail leaving a home, or a source of livelihood or a family
to go to a new place. Certainly many of the first followers
of Jesus fulfilled his calling in this sense by taking the good
news to new people and places. However, there could also
be a wider interpretation of what being an 'apostle' (sent
one) means. As well as leaving something physically behind,
it could also entail a changed direction of the will, a new
motivation and a freedom from past limitations. In other
words, the call of Jesus is to broadened horizons, away from
the securities of the past with its fixed assumptions and
limited perceptions. This sense of apostleship is helpful to us
all, whatever the circumstances of our lives.

Among the followers of Jesus, Mary Magdalene can be
taken as an example of an 'apostle' in this broad sense of the
word. In her call Jesus gave a sense of dignity and purpose
to Mary's life that would have been rare among women of
the day. Although from our perspective we might wish that
Jesus had called women to number among the twelve, there
can be no doubting the radical challenge to gender expectations that Jesus created. Mary is numbered among those
who travelled about with Jesus as he went from place to
place 'bringing the good news of the kingdom of God'
(Luke 8.1). In this passage Luke mentions by name
Mary Magdalene and two other women (Joanna and
Susanna) in addition to the twelve. As well as introducing
Mary Magdalene Luke tells the reader that seven demons
had gone out from her. However we interpret the deliver-
ance ministry of Jesus, freedom from the past and for the
future is central: 'So if anyone is in Christ, there is a new
creation: everything old has passed away; see, everything
has become new!' (2 Cor. 5.17).

This is a pre-resurrection appearance of Mary. According
to John's Gospel she is the first to encounter the risen
Christ and she is also found in Matthew 28.1. The account
in John's Gospel of the encounter of Mary Magdalene with
the risen Jesus demonstrates the expanding of horizons that

is implicit to the first disciples' experience of calling. Mary at first fails to recognize Jesus, but as he calls her by name her mind and heart already begin to stretch to experience him in this radically new way. But this marks the beginning of the expanding of Mary's horizons and she is still tempted to hold to Jesus – to relate to him according to the expectations of their friendship prior to his death. In response Jesus turns Mary's love and joy outwards as she becomes the first witness to the resurrection: 'Mary Magdalene went and announced to the disciples, "I have seen the Lord"' (John 20.18). Mary demonstrates two essential hallmarks of authentic Christian vocation:

- A willingness to explore and embrace new and richer expressions of a relationship with Jesus, even when this means abandoning old and cherished understandings.
- A willingness to express this relationship by sharing it with others and allowing them to be caught up in this 'apostolic' movement.

The final characteristic of authentic Christian ministry that we will explore from the first followers of Jesus is their identification with the suffering and death of Jesus. More will be said in the second part of this chapter, as in the period before the death of Jesus there is an almost universal failure on the part of the disciples to accept and embrace Jesus' need to suffer. From the strength of Jesus' reaction to Peter when he rebukes predictions of suffering and death we can see that Peter's response is regarded by Jesus as a failing in discipleship.

If any want to become my followers, let them deny themselves and take up their cross and follow me.

Matthew 16.24

Mary's anointing of Jesus' feet with costly ointment as an anticipation of his death suggests a willingness to embrace his fate not shared by any of her fellow disciples:

> *Six days before the Passover Jesus came to Bethany, the home of Lazarus, whom he had raised from the dead. There they gave a dinner for him. Martha served, and Lazarus was one of those at the table with him. Mary took a pound of costly perfume made of pure nard, anointed Jesus' feet, and wiped them with her hair. The house was filled with the fragrance of the perfume. But Judas Iscariot, one of the disciples (the one who was about to betray him) said, 'Why was this perfume not sold for three hundred denarii and the money given to the poor?' (He said this not because he cared about the poor, but because he was a thief; he kept the common purse and used to steal what was put into it.) Jesus said, 'Leave her alone. She bought it so that she might keep it for the day of my burial. You always have the poor with you, but you do not always have me.'*
>
> John 12.1–8

After Pentecost all this would change as many of the disciples literally shared Jesus' suffering and death.

Ministry in the early Church

The event and experience of Pentecost transformed the ministry of the disciples of Jesus, giving them boldness in proclaiming the good news and courage in the face of persecution. The gift of the Spirit at Pentecost was none other than the Spirit of Jesus, enabling his followers to have a closer than ever identification with him. No longer simply companions and friends of Jesus they were now 'in Christ' as Paul later described it (2 Cor. 5.17). The calling to reflect the life and ministry of Jesus was now animated by the indwelling presence of Christ.

The patterns of ministry and leadership within the early

Church continue to be widely discussed by New Testament scholars, and much of the debate centres around how these patterns relate to ministry within the Church today. Without getting into these debates the evidence of the Acts of the Apostles and the Epistles suggests that patterns varied from place to place and that a range of ministries and callings was celebrated.

In his description of spiritual gifts and ministry within the Church, Paul tells the Corinthians that the various forms of service are all manifestations of the one Spirit given for the common good. The gifts and ministries are allotted to each individual as the Spirit chooses. Although this seems entirely random, our own experience tells us that our different personalities and abilities are often used by God in the calling given to each of us. Occasionally the Spirit will enable someone to perform a task or fulfil a calling that seems to go against the grain of their natural aptitude and ability; but more often God will build on our natural talents and dispositions in the gifts and ministries we are given. As we saw earlier, each person is called to reflect the life and ministry of Jesus in their own particular and unique ways – 'but it is the same God who activates all of them in everyone' (1 Cor. 12.6).

It is a cause for rejoicing that there has been a new emphasis upon every-member ministry within the Church in recent generations. Particular callings, such as to ordained ministry, need to be seen in their proper context of the sharing of ministry within the Body of Christ. Paul makes it quite clear that no ministry, and no individual, can be dispensed with without everyone suffering.

Treasure in clay jars

In the first part of this chapter we recognized that we are called even with our own particular personal histories, limitations and failings. This reality is expressed powerfully by Paul in his image of 'treasure in clay jars' (2 Cor. 4.7). When Paul is at his most autobiographical his own personal sense of inadequacy and weakness is most plain. He recognizes that his life in Christ and his ministry as an apostle depend absolutely upon the mercy of God. Through this mercy God 'has shone in our hearts to give the light of the knowledge of the glory of God in the face of Jesus Christ' (2 Cor. 4.6). This is the treasure contained within the 'clay jars' of our ordinary and often broken lives. Awareness of personal limitation and brokenness was a source of liberation for Paul, enabling him to know that the life of Jesus may be made visible in our mortal flesh.

Henri Nouwen

Henri Nouwen was a Dutch Roman Catholic priest, academic and well-known author. From being professor at Harvard Divinity School he came to live among people with developmental disabilities at the L'Arche Daybreak Community in Canada, an experience which he describes as a home-coming, although he also recognized that he spent much time and energy fleeing this 'home' for which he longed. Carolyn Whitney Brown, a member of L'Arche Daybreak, describes Henri Nouwen as someone 'very gifted and very broken' and identifies a 'chaotic inner life, the emotional struggles and needs he could recognize but not change, his fears, busyness, enormous self-centredness, his aching loneliness . . . and also the sacred space around Henri's heart where he freely welcomed anyone who needed him'.

Such a sense of liberation has been shared by many in the history of the Church and is powerfully captured by Henri Nouwen's notion of being a 'Wounded Healer'.[2] Part of the courage of Christian vocation is to acknowledge and identify personal weaknesses as well as strengths, and to offer them in our service of Christ.

Suffering for Christ

The really significant distinction between the pre- and post-Pentecost period was the willingness of the disciples not only to accept that the suffering and death of Jesus were necessary for our salvation, but also to embrace this spirit of sacrifice for themselves. The persecution and martyrdom of Christians is a refrain throughout the Acts of the Apostles and has continued relatively unabated in one part of the world or another ever since. However, many of us are not in such a situation where our life or freedom is threatened by our discipleship and we are left wondering what it means for us to be 'carrying in the body the death of Jesus' (2 Cor. 4.10).

> We are afflicted in every way, but not crushed; perplexed, but not driven to despair; persecuted, but not forsaken; struck down, but not destroyed.
>
> 2 Corinthians 4.8–9

To respond to the call of Christ will entail different challenges for each individual, but there will almost certainly be some cost attached, because ministry in all forms entails an identification with the suffering and death of Jesus. Paul speaks of his own sufferings as the genuine hallmark of his ministry as an apostle, and he offers them as an example of true discipleship to the churches. Even for Paul the suffering could take many forms.

Far from presenting a portrayal of calling that is unique to the first followers of Jesus, their discipleship provides a model for our own. Their example is both encouraging and challenging at the same time; and they urge us to be imitators of Christ.

Some questions

1 How can our personalities, and even our weaknesses and failings, contribute to our vocation?
2 What can we do together, and what do we do together, to reflect the life of Christ?
3 What might it mean in your own situation to identify in your own callings the suffering and death of Jesus?

CHAPTER 6

The Call through Baptism

Sheila Nunn

The journey of discipleship takes many pathways and many doors. Most significantly we journey, or are carried, through the door of a church. Within the Christian community the meaning of our discipleship (whether we understand it or not) is rehearsed and proclaimed through baptism. It is a liturgical journey, but one which sheds much light on the rest of our lives.

Imagine a church where the baptism of a baby is about to take place. The family and guests are gathered, the font gently steams with warm water, some of the symbolic artefacts are laid ready and the priest is waiting for the parents to bring their baby. This is the scene played out countless times every Sunday in churches throughout the world. It appears to be such a simple ceremony – a few prayers, some water, maybe some oil and a candle. Yet it is the supreme moment of our calling to follow Christ and become members of his Body – the Church. The symbols of baptism carry with them many layers of meaning. They signify an introduction into a particular way of life and symbolize the Christian community and our part in it.

In marriage two people are called into relationship by the declaration of their intent before God and the people assembled. Just as marriage is a public declaration of what two people hope to be to each other and to the wider community, so baptism declares God's unwavering love for each part of his creation. During the celebration the parents hold the child to present it to the community because their child is a living symbol of their love and commitment to each other. A baby is an outward and visible sign of parental love and could be said to be a sacrament in itself. Baptism is just such a sign of the love between God and his people. God holds us each as a precious child.

As they stand with the child, fruit of their love, the parents publicly reaffirm their love and commitment and they bring the child for acceptance by God and the Christian community. Thus begins a calling and a life of acceptance, responsibility and commitment. This public declaration will be revisited at confirmation when we are called as adults to declare our faith and receive our com-mission into the work of the Kingdom of God. There may be other times and occasions in our adult lives when we are called to say what we believe in front of others and what we understand has happened at our baptism.

It is valuable to consider some of the elements of baptism and see how they relate to our calling as the people of God.

Water

Water is the most significant element of baptism. The symbolism of washing reminds us of the flawed nature into which we were born. Water brings cleanliness, an oppor-tunity to become a new person with sin washed away. This image is sometimes hard to reconcile with the innocence of a baby but it reflects accurately the inevitability of the future – that merely by being human we will make mistakes and be less than perfect.

The gushing waters of birth as the child leaves the womb signal a new relationship with the world. Through the baptismal water we are called into a new relationship with God and the world.

The baptismal prayer over the water in the font reflects a journey. The words echo our salvation history as the people of God – God's holy people. This symbolism resonates with our experience and understanding: we are called from the chaos of the waters of creation to the new life in Christ. We are called on a journey, a pilgrimage. The world was called into being from the waters of chaos; Noah was called to follow God and was saved from the flood waters. Moses led the people of God from their old lives of slavery in Egypt, through the waters of the Red Sea, to new lives of freedom in the promised land. Jesus was baptized in the river Jordan by John and called to move on from Nazareth to preach, teach, heal the sick and to call people to follow him. At his baptism his identity was affirmed by the seal of the Holy Spirit, empowering him to respond to God's call. The words remind us that later he passed through the deep waters of death to resurrection to new life. And Paul saw baptism as our dying (drowning) en route to our resurrection (Rom. 6.1–11).

Through baptism we are called to follow him, through death to our former selves to a resurrected life of helping to bring in God's Kingdom. Even this baby is called and commissioned into its ministry as a follower of Jesus – a Christian.

Newly clothed

It may be in the next part of the service that the child (who may have been liberally covered with water) will be reclothed. This is another powerful symbol of what our calling at baptism is all about. We leave behind the clothes we were wearing, symbols of the old person we were. We are called to be separate from the world yet to live in it and so we receive new clothes – the christening robe. Here the symbol is of 'putting on the Lord Jesus Christ' in Paul's words (Rom. 13.14): we wear the uniform of Christ in order to become like him and are called to be holy, set apart.

Newly named

At baptism the priest may ask the parents what name they have given their child. This has a practical purpose in making sure that the priest names the child correctly but it has a theological significance as well. In Chapter One of this book we looked at the call through creation and how we are linked with God's creative act in naming all creation. To name is to know and recognize. We see what St Paul says about baptism in his Letter to the Romans. Paul explains to his readers that since they have received the Spirit of God through baptism they are no longer limited by life in the flesh but alive in the Spirit, because the Spirit of Christ dwells in them and they are part of Christ's resurrected life. Through the indwelling of the Spirit they have become adopted sons and daughters of the Father and have the right to call him 'Abba'. Through the outpouring of the Spirit, they have become joint-heirs with Christ.

Do you not know that all of us who have been baptized into Christ Jesus were baptized into his death? There we have been buried with him by baptism into death, so that, just as Christ was raised from the dead by the glory of the Father, so we too might walk in newness of life.

For if we have been united with him in a death like his, we will certainly be united with him in a resurrection like his. We know that our old self was crucified with him so that the body of sin might no longer be enslaved to sin. For whoever has died is freed from sin. But if we have died with Christ, we believe that we will also live with him. We know that Christ, being raised from the dead, will never die again; death no longer has dominion over him. The death he died, he died to sin, once for all; but the life he lives, he lives to God. So you also must consider yourselves dead to sin and alive to God in Christ Jesus.

Romans 6.3–11

In Romans Chapter 6 Paul states that the call through baptism implies that we may be called to suffer with Christ. Through our baptism we are buried with Christ in his death and rise with him to new life – the resurrected life. We are called to life in all its fullness and will live after death with Christ.

> So then, brothers and sisters, we are debtors, not to the flesh, to live according to the flesh – for if you live according to the flesh, you will die; but if by the Spirit you put to death the deeds of the body, you will live. For all who are led by the Spirit of God are children of God. For you did not receive a spirit of slavery to fall back into fear, but you have received a spirit of adoption. When we cry, 'Abba! Father!' it is that very Spirit bearing witness with our spirit that we are children of God, and if children, then heirs, heirs of God and joint heirs with Christ – if, in fact, we suffer with him so that we may also be glorified with him.
>
> Romans 8.12–17

Oil

To return to our imaginary church and the newly baptized and clothed baby, we now come to the anointing. The oil is blessed by the Bishop on Maundy Thursday. Sometimes the oil of Chrism is used – olive oil to which sweet-smelling perfume has been added. The Holy Spirit has been given to the child through the water of baptism and the oil signifies the recognition or seal of the Spirit. Chrism is used also in the ordination of priests and symbolizes the priesthood of all believers. We are all called to share in the priesthood of Christ and we are confirmed as God's adopted sons and daughters. Chrism is used too in the anointing of a monarch, from Solomon onwards, and is used in coronations today. It bestows royalty so we are

all made 'royal' princesses and princes by anointing. The
word 'Christ' means the 'anointed one' and so we are
anointed like Jesus in order to follow him. But the anointing of priests or royalty signifies not only that they are given
regal status but also that they are called to serve. Baptism
brings with it a responsibility to be the servant of others
and to help the Kingdom to grow.

---

*Meanwhile Saul, still breathing threats and murder against the dis-
ciples of the Lord, went to the high priest and asked him for letters to
the synagogues at Damascus, so that if he found any who belonged to
the Way, men or women, he might bring them bound to Jerusalem.
Now as he was going along and approaching Damascus, suddenly a
light from heaven flashed around him. He fell to the ground and
heard a voice saying to him, 'Saul, Saul, why do you persecute me?'
He asked, 'Who are you, Lord?' The reply came, 'I am Jesus, whom you
are persecuting. But get up and enter the city, and you will be told
what you are to do.' The men who were travelling with him stood
speechless because they heard the voice but saw no one. Saul got up
from the ground, and though his eyes were open, he could see nothing;
so they led him by the hand and brought him into Damascus.*

Acts 9.1–8

At Pentecost the disciples were sealed by the Spirit and
called out from their ordinary lives to tell the world about
Jesus and his redeeming love. In Acts (9.1–31) we read of
what happened to Paul. He met Jesus on the Damascus road
and was temporarily blinded and led into the city. He
turned from trying to kill Jesus' followers to believing in
him but it was not until he was welcomed by the Christian
community and incorporated into it that he became a great
missionary, taking the gospel into much of the known
world. In his time the early Church was known as 'the Way'
so to be baptized into the group was to be called to a
journey, to join others on 'the Way', the way to bring in

God's Kingdom of justice and peace. So through baptism
we are all called to share the gospel wherever we are, in
whatever circumstances. It is a mistake to think that it is
only the specialized task of those who are ordained.

Light

In baptism we are given the light. During the ceremony the
Paschal candle, symbol of Christ's resurrection, is lit and at
the end of the service a small candle is given to the child via
the parents and godparents. The child through baptism is no
longer in a dark world, but connected to Jesus' resurrection from the dead. Jesus called himself the light of the
world and the parents and godparents, holding their child's
candle, lit from the Paschal candle, are encouraged to hold
the light as they hold the light of faith for this child. It will
be their responsibility to make sure that it is not extin-
guished. We are called to be lights in the world that shine in
our own particular place to the glory of God. Each of us
through baptism has a part to play in guarding the light and
passing it on to others.

> Again Jesus spoke to them, saying, 'I am the light of the world.
> Whoever follows me will never walk in darkness but will have the
> light of life.'
>
> John 8.12

A welcome

The Christian community is called into discipleship and
service, individually and communally. Thus the newly baptized are given a welcome that is both personal and public,
a welcome which expects the presence of God in the lives of
all people. Being called by baptism into discipleship means

our learning to worship with the Church, to grow in prayer, to listen to the scriptures and to serve our neighbour as ourselves.

The Church's call
To see itself as a baptised people
to welcome and learn from the enquirer
to be active in mission and service
to expect the anointing of the Holy Spirit
to walk with those seeking faith
to stand with the despised and oppressed
to look for the unity of God's people.[1]

The newly baptized is greeted by the community as it is made explicit that we are on a common journey:

Today God has touched you with his love
and given you a place among his people.
God promises to be with you
in joy and in sorrow,
to be your guide for life,
and to bring you safely to heaven.
In baptism God invites you on a life-long journey.
Together with all God's people
you must explore the way of Jesus
and grow in friendship with God,
in love for his people
and in serving others.
With us you will listen to the word of God
and receive the gifts of God.[2]

We leave our imaginary group as they lead the way to the door with the baptismal candle, carrying the newly baptized child, received into God's family, sealed with his

Holy Spirit, clothed in the garments of Christ. Over the years they will nurture and watch this child grow. They will keep the light, lit as a guiding light, until the child is old enough to respond to God's call. The call is to ministry in its widest sense; to follow in the Way, to be acknowledged and named as a unique individual and to be part of a community. It is to this calling that we respond, whatever our circumstances.

Some questions

1 In what ways do you feel that you are responding to your baptismal promises?
2 How can we fulfil our baptism calling? What helps to determine the place God has for us in his scheme of things?
3 Is there a place for the baptism of the children of non-churchgoing families?

CHAPTER 7

The Calling of the Church

Christopher Burke

God's call is unique to each of us but God rarely calls us to a solitary life. We are called into communities, for particular purposes in the world. In their own ways local communities and churches take on unique roles. These communities have diverse characteristics but a common bond in responding collectively to what God wants for the world.

While it is relatively easy for us to be aware of individual and personal vocation, it may be less easy for us to sense the vocation of the Church as a whole. Sometimes, we may over-emphasize our personal sense of vocation, and lose sight of the collective vocation of the Church. The context of the modern Church is full of examples where the individual takes primacy over the community, in a world where even politicians struggle with the concept of community; and that secular pressure will inevitably have an impact on our own perceptions.

The vocation of each individual and the vocation of the Church, while distinctive, are strongly bound and are interdependent, because we are called to live within and as communities. It is clear that the Church has a vocation, manifested in the example of the apostles, the life of early Christian communities, and in generations of communal faithful witness. It is almost inevitable that all those who participate in the life of local churches will have been shaped and affected by the response of that community in understanding its own history within the parish. We can see this clearly in how the vocation of the Church develops in relation to changes in its context; and then, in turn, the vocation of the individual is shaped by the way that the Church understands its calling to serve the wider community.

Call to mission

St James' Church is in a rural market town facing enormous change and that has seen a great degree of difficulty over recent years. The town and church are struggling with rising unemployment and wrestling with a downturn in the local economy and with the corresponding effect on community life. St James' Church is Anglo-Catholic by tradition; its current vicar has been at the church for about three years. She sees mission as a central part of the life and nature of the church.

St James' Church has for a number of years been through a process of discernment and reflection. Using times away from the parish and a lengthy period of reflection, the various groups within the parish set about trying to listen to how God was calling them.

As a result they followed a call to active mission within the local community that lasted for a number of years. Throughout the whole experience many in the church community were very aware that God had called them and was sustaining and enabling their efforts to bear some clear fruit.

Following the mission activities, the growing and changing church community again sought to listen to God as they began to put together a Mission Action Plan, involving wide-ranging consultation, participation across the church community and the ownership of most of those connected with the Church.

Even though there was a variety of opinions, after a period of time the members of the church were able to come together united in their hope to follow a common calling.

A changing vocation?

In some communities the Church may express its vocation to work with the poor and the marginalized; in others, it may seek to minister to those who have the power to bring

change to a troubled world. As churches are shaped by their
historical and social context, so too the sense of vocation in
that church will be shaped. Churches which once stood
splendidly at the heart of prosperous industrial or rural life
now find they are ministering to some of the poorest and
most socially deprived communities. In these cases, the
understanding of the vocation of the Church, and the way
it is expressed in that area, are clearly moulded by context.
As the context continues to change and unfold, so does the
vocation of the Church in that place.

In order to reflect on the vocation of the Church, it
might be helpful to reflect on its principal activities. The
primary function of the Church is expressed in its corporate pattern of continuous worship and prayer. There is a
strong sense that the Church prays a liturgy and pattern of
prayer which is common, and is used with degrees of
variety throughout Christian communities of the world. In
its commitment to prayer and worship we find in the
Church a universal enthusiasm, which runs against so many
of the things that seem to divide us.

> If you do not join in what the church is doing, you have no share in
> this Spirit. For where the church is, there is the Spirit of God; and
> where the Spirit of God is, there is the church and every kind of
> grace. [1]

Such a pattern of prayer and worship is maintained
locally, and Christians find themselves participating in that
rhythm which lies at the heart of so many church communities. Whether it is through a commitment to the daily
Eucharist and Daily Office, or through more informal gath-
erings, common and regular prayer is the universal practice
of the Church. Indeed it is hard to imagine how the Church
could be itself without it.

For some people the mission of the Church provides a clear focus for the life of the community. There is then a strong sense of the mission of the Church being a particular manifestation of its vocation. We have all been affected by the Church's understanding of mission, as the continuing tangible expression of God's love to the world. That makes it, of course, not our individual mission, nor even the Church's, but rather, how we share in the divine desire for the world to know and experience God's love and grace – it is indeed God's mission. Church communities seek to reach out to those who do not yet know the gospel; and the Church attaches a high priority to this mission. For some it is necessary simply to secure continuation of the church community; for others it is the very essence of what the Church is called to be – engaged with the task of helping others to know for themselves the love and grace of God.

Many Christians are conscious that the Church of today is the product of the faithful mission of earlier generations of communities and individuals. But for their labours, the life of the Church would be very different. Mission has been a clear and legitimate expression of the Church's vocation throughout history.

The variety of callings

The Church seeks to be faithful in its vocation to make the gospel known within many varied contexts and communities. There are bound to be differences in the ways in which that vocation is expressed when churches live in different social, economic and ethnic contexts. One of the great challenges to the Church is the need to be flexible and versatile while maintaining integrity to its vocation. Within the Anglican Communion alone, we find a variety of expression shaped by the context in which the Church is at work: active Christian presence within the institutions of government and privilege, and within deprived and socially challenged inner cities; in the child-friendly family service, and in cathedral choral evensong; in predominantly white, middle-class suburbia; and in the widely spread villages of the African continent. If variety is the spice of life, then there is clearly much of it in the Church.

The vocation of the Church, expressed in pastoral ministry, seeks to develop the local community of faith. For many, it is the experience of this ministry that initially brings them into the life of the worshipping community and helps them feel that they belong. Increasingly the Church is affirming the pastoral ministry of lay people, often specifically authorized as an expression of the pastoral vocation of the Church itself. It is clear from the scriptures that the early Church had a pastoral heart, and such a calling is still expressed today.

All of us will have experienced ways in which the Church seeks to be faithful to its calling, and how we understand that to be a rather different vocation from that of an individual. The two may well overlap, however, as we see when we consider the vocation of those who exercise an ordained ministry in the Church. The ordination service relates how the new deacon or priest is to function within the life of the Church. Clergy are a focal point for the ministry of the whole church community and an expression of its catholicity. They bring to their ministry a variety of gifts and abilities, which will be different from that of their peers, and yet they are clearly expressing their ministry within the Church of God as a whole.

Hearing God's call

St Saviour's Church is in a large city centre and it draws people from all over the city. Consequently it brings together people from a wide range of traditions and with a variety of experiences. It has managed to hold together both the charismatic and Catholic, and seeks to be faithful through a life of prayer and teaching, which, it is hoped, will lead to action within the local community.

St Saviour's Church had been hoping to hear God's call for some time and a group was well established which spent time regularly praying and seeking to listen to God.

At one such meeting, following a prayer asking that God might speak to those present, the silence was broken by a homeless man asking very loudly if anybody had a light for his cigarette. The response of those gathered was to tell the man to go away because they were praying. Later, the group recognized God's call in that experience, and the church opened a very successful day centre for the homeless and others in need.

There was a realization by the church that the call of God is not always as subtle as some of the ways that we try to seek God's call.

What kind of community?

The vocation of the Church must be seen to inform the vocation of the individual. We are all called within the community of the Church, but the individual vocation should also be expressed within the life of the world. Just as God has formed and called the Church to serve the world, so too the individual Christian is called to that service, whether as lay people or ordained. Even those who are called to a solitary life express that vocation within the greater context of the Church in the world.

Right from the start, Jesus created a strong sense of community in his ministry with his disciples. There were times for prayer, discussion and reflection; times, doubtless, for fun and recreation; and times for serious, hard work. Those who were sent out went from one community to another community, and returned home again. Those who answered Jesus' call to follow him were called out of their everyday lives and into a new community of those who had been called and had responded.

St Paul's letters place a high value on the Christian

community and on the calling of the Church. Indeed, the accounts we have of those who sustained the earliest churches by their teaching, preaching and encouragement help us to develop a sense of Church transcending local and national boundaries. This gives us a vision of Christian communities which are different from the one to which we may belong. St Paul's writings often focus on the building of church community and on the dangers of division. Some of the churches to whom he directed his remarks and devoted his time were clearly at risk of crumbling, and yet he encourages them in recognizing the value and import-ance of the common life, the need for reconciliation, and a proper focus on their vocation. His imagery of there being many parts to the one body, and the cohesive nature of the whole, is something that St Paul seeks to give particular value: we were made to be in community, and it is as such that the love we seek to share and proclaim finds its most fruitful expression.

In the Acts of the Apostles we read how that first fellow-ship shared in common and met together for prayers and the breaking of the bread. Perhaps this is a somewhat ideal-ized picture of the life of the Church, but it remains a powerful model of community life in which members share themselves, their gifts, money and resources with each other. While it may be seen worked out today in religious communities living under the same roof, there are valid principles also for a local church.

> *Now the whole group of those who believed were of one heart and soul, and no one claimed private ownership of any possessions, but everything they owned was held in common. With great power the apostles gave their testimony to the resurrection of the Lord Jesus and great grace was upon them all.*
>
> Acts 4.32–3

Promoting community life does not have to mean uniformity. Distinctiveness and individuality are a beneficial element in the gifts that we can offer. Despite the Church's collective vocation, there is still scope for the expression of the individual's vocation. We are not called all to be the same, nor necessarily to do the same things, but to offer our own distinctive gifts to the fulfilment of the whole.

What kind of Church?

Our understanding of the Church's vocation is inevitably affected by our awareness of what we believe it ought to mean to be a member of the community of God's people. Looking at different models of the Church may help to identify positive and life-giving forms of vocation; as well as those which are less creative and better to avoid.

- For some, the Church is seen, even from within, as an authoritative and sometimes oppressive institution which regulates and restricts the freedom of the individual. This will shape in a particular way the understanding of personal vocation and ministry. Some Christians are at ease with this ordered and tidy style which offers a degree of certainty in matters of faith and discipline. The acceptance of clearly defined rules and regulations within the community will foster equally definite individual vocations, where to toe the party line is a yardstick of firm faith and orthodoxy. It may also stifle the will of the individual to think creatively and imaginatively, about themselves, about those beyond the community, and about matters where the wider Church is clearly not of one mind. Communities like these are often very clear about where they stand on a wide variety of issues, and those who do not conform, or who question the leadership view, run the risk of feeling marginalized and living with a sense of guilt, unworthiness or dissatisfaction, which in turn will limit the potential of personal vocation.

- There are also churches which lack confidence in the face of the challenge to engage with twenty-first-century culture and society. They are defensive of the past, perhaps clinging to the memory of what they see as happier times, and are reluctant to adapt. Within such communities, the hope, expectation and joy of fresh individual and communal vocation is likely to be swamped by scepticism and pessimism, and they are unlikely to be attractive to those with new vision, or to welcome their presence.
- There are churches which are fiercely democratic, where everything is decided by the sub-committees and by the PCC, with every individual having the accepted right to speak and be heard. Sometimes this is a creative and fruitful way for a church to take decisions, but it can also be a source of frustration and division. The Church of God is littered with breakaway groups and sects, set up following decisions that were not acceptable to a minority. Where consensus and agreement are pursued extensively in order to disenfranchise no one, discerning the vocation of the church may take a very long time.

Alongside these types or models of Christian community sits the greater part of the Church, holding together in unity an untidy and varied range of ecclesiology, experience, outlook and practice. The nature of the community has an impact not only on the way in which the Church identifies its call, but also on the freedom of those within it to express their own vocation within that church community.

What kind of discipleship?

It has been important to recognize that the vocation of both the Church and the individual are closely related and affecting each other; and that both will be shaped by the context of individual and collective ministry. Sometimes the local church will enable and affirm the individual's experience of vocation; at other times the individual may be stifled by either the apparent strength or the apparent weakness of the community.

This raises relevant questions not only about the authenticity of the individual's vocation but also about the nature and ministry of the home church. Our own vocation nearly always comes from within the context of the Church, and those pursuing their own sense of vocation need to be aware of that as an important part of the discernment process. The Church will wish to have a formal part to play in testing vocations, particularly to the ordained ministry. Such involvement should be seen as creative and positive, even if ultimately there are different perceptions of the individual vocation.

Some questions

1 In what ways has your personal response to the vocation of the Church enriched your own individual areas of ministry?
2 How has your experience of the ministry of the Church shaped the understanding of your own vocation?
3 In what ways have you experienced your local church as either restricting or enabling your sense of vocation?

CHAPTER 8

The Call to Pray and Work

Judith Gray, CSC

In daily living, and daily dying, we find our discipleship.
We are called to do extraordinary things, often in a very
ordinary setting. But the ordinary setting of daily life
contains a jewel of great worth: the belief that, mysteri-
ously and wonderfully, God makes himself at home with
us – in our work, our prayer and our relationships.

The case for McDonald's

The founder of McDonald's is purported to have stated, 'At home, I believe in God, my family and McDonald's. When I go to the office I reverse the order.' We might wonder if he would have been commended by the apostle Paul who wrote to the folk at Colossae, 'Whatever your task, put yourselves into it, as done for the Lord' (Col. 3.23). Perhaps he would (setting aside for the moment questions that occur to us about 'fast food' in general), for the apostle said elsewhere, 'we were not idle when we were with you . . . but with toil and labour we worked night and day' (2 Thess. 3.7b–8b), and 'anyone unwilling to work should not eat' (2 Thess. 3.10)!

> *My Father is still working, and I also am working.*
>
> John 5.17

This begs the question of the unemployed, those retrenched for no fault of their own, and those whom excessive work destroys, but in general it seems to encapsulate a truth. For we know that being human is inseparable from the life of work. Our faith as Christians commits us to the belief that the God who created the entire universe never ceases to work on and within it; and we are to be co-workers, co-creators with God.

> *I glorified you on earth by finishing the work that you gave me to do.*
>
> John 17.4

Like the rest of humankind, our life as Christians will entail work of some kind. Although the truth-filled myths at the beginning of Genesis tell us that hard toil is a punishment for our disobedience, work actually gives us a sense of identity, dignity and purpose. Paid employment, say the sociologists, is one of the quantifiably most satisfying ways of spending one's days. Those without paid work can feel frustrated and demeaned, without a sense of self-worth and self-respect. Even the humblest work can be made purposeful if, for example, it supports one's family and can be recognized as a service to society, to other people.

Brother Lawrence

Brother Lawrence, a seventeenth-century French monk and author of a little classic, The Practice of the Presence of God, *worked in the kitchen of his Burgundian monastery. His work was neither glamorous nor high flying, but he exuded a sense of contentment and maturity. Engaged in menial tasks and clumsy into the bargain, he yet seemed to have a solid sense of his own identity and value in God's eyes, as well as a worthwhile purpose and usefulness in feeding the Brothers! Everyone, sooner or later, wants to find purpose in their occupation; those who work in the service industries no less than the rest of the workforce.*

The life-promoting gospel

If the gospel of Jesus Christ is really good news, then it will have to address us as workers, as people involved fully in human life, for Jesus calls us, not to religion, but to life, life irradiated by faith:

> *I came that they may have life, and have it abundantly.*
> John 10.10

An early Church Father, Irenaeus (AD 130–200), who was Bishop of Lyons in France, seems to understand the import of Jesus' words since he claims, 'The glory of God is a human being fully alive.'[1] He also thought that if we conformed ourselves to the divine order of things, we would come to share God's glory. Part of that divine order is the necessity of human work, and if the gospel is life-enhancing it must have something to say about our daily lives and work however humdrum and ordinary. For it is in our daily lives that we are to find God, be found of God and give glory to God. We may feel them to be too ordinary, that we need a different set of circumstances, or work that seems more directly an expression of our faith. Perhaps, as we shall see later on, we will be called to make changes, but the place to begin is in life as it is, here and now.

The sacrament of daily life and work

In Chapter One of this book we read, 'God speaks to us through the language of everyday events. Each new moment or situation holds a clue to God's call and we will always find our call in the circumstances and experiences of daily life.' Now this makes our life very exciting, full of possibilities. Jürgen Moltmann said in a lecture in 1998 that it is as if 'the experience of the eternal God brings our own temporal life . . . into an ocean that surrounds and supports us when we swim in it'.[2]

We may ask: Do you really mean *my* life in my suburban semi, battling with the mortgage and the children? It is hard to value our own lives sometimes and see them as the theatre of God's presence and activity. There is a saying of Jesus from the Apocryphal Gospel of Thomas, 'Split the wood and I am there. Lift the stone and you will find me.'[4] Going about their daily work, the woodcutter and the stonemason will encounter the living Christ. Searching within our own work will reveal the same Christ.

Seeing God in everyday life
There was once a little fish who was always longing to find the ocean. One day the little fish met an older, wiser fish to whom he said, 'Excuse me, you are older than I, can you tell me where to find this thing they call the ocean?' 'The ocean,' said the older fish, 'is the thing you are in now.' 'Oh, this?' said the little fish very disappointed. 'But this is only water.' Stop searching little fish. There isn't anything to look for. All you have to do is look.[3]

How would that translate into your daily life and work? Since Jesus calls us to life, to be fully human, everything can become a means of grace to us – washing up, cleaning the car, computing, feeding the animals, caring in a thousand ways in workplace or at home. Wise and experienced followers of Jesus encourage us to believe that our salvation begins always on the level of common and natural and ordinary things, in the sacramentality of daily life – making coffee, preparing meals, taking a shower.[5] A greatly loved Anglican priest and poet, George Herbert (1593–1633) put it this way:

Teach me, my God and King,
In all things Thee to see,
And what I do in anything
To do it as for Thee.[6]

This way of looking at things, of seeing God in all things,
needs cultivating. It can transform what feels like the dreari-
ness of daily life into something creative and purposeful,
even delightful! Starting the day with deliberate intention,
with a morning offering of the day to God, can be a good
way to begin it. Depending on our circumstances we need
to give time, however short, to it. It can be as simple as,
'My God, here is this day, fill it with your presence,
strength and love. Let all I do be done with you.' If you say,
'I have no time', make the offering in your own words as
you clean your teeth or sit on the bus or train. The important thing is to *make* it, not *where* it is made.

O Lord! thou knowest how busy I must be this day: if I forget thee, do
not thou forget me.[7]

Others will find that they can spend more time and
perhaps add to the simple offering a short reading from the
Gospels asking: How can this passage be applied to my life
today? The directing of a new day towards God is very
important. Our Celtic forebears regarded even the act of
waking up each morning as a gift. In the prayer attributed
to St Patrick, *The Deer's Cry* (overleaf), God's presence is
invoked in words of great power and beauty. Receiving the
gift of each new day in such a positive spirit, we can be sure
that holiness may be found in doing the next thing we have
to do with our whole heart and even find delight in doing
it.

> **The Deer's Cry**
> *I arise today*
> *Through God's strength to direct me,*
> *God's might to uphold me,*
> *God's wisdom to guide me,*
> *God's eye to look before,*
> *God's ear to hear me,*
> *God's word to speak to me,*
> *God's hand to guard me,*
> *God's way to lie before me,*
> *God's shield to protect me.*[8]

The great twentieth-century Jesuit palaeontologist, Pierre Teilhard de Chardin, seems to take the encouragement even further: 'God awaits us every instant in our action, in the work of the moment. There is a sense in which God is at the tip of my pen, my spade, my brush, my needle, of my heart and of my thought.'[9] We could add among other things, 'and at my keyboard and computer screen'.

The point is that God is present waiting for us as we work. In so far as we carry our work to its completion, its ultimate finish, our efforts are made holy, we are united to God. Now this happens, whether or not we think about it at that moment; the morning offering has turned our heart towards God. Our compass has been set for the day with all its occupations, whatever the day may bring.

The heavenly kaleidoscope

As members of the human family and specifically of the Christian family, we know that we are wrapped up in the bundle of life with many others, a bit like God's kaleidoscope. Here are all those little pieces of coloured glass, all different sizes, shapes and colours, and as the kaleidoscope moves, they make patterns which change all the time. All of them are needed to complete the mandalas that evolve.

The writer of the Letter to the Ephesians gives us a similar picture: 'There is one body and one Spirit'; 'each of us was given grace according to the measure of Christ's gift' (4.1–13). Then Paul lists some of the gifts and workers we find in Christ's Body, the Church: apostles, prophets, pastors, teachers and others.

We may quite rightly feel that we don't come into that category. What about hairdressers, cleaners, check-out staff, mechanics, engineers, farmers, accountants, IT experts? Can Christians see any value in doing these jobs? (It may be some consolation to know that in the early Church other functionaries were mentioned, like doorkeepers!) They may not seem directly linked with our religion. But maybe we too can be apostles (those commissioned and sent into our workplace), prophets and evangelists, speaking out in our workplace, speaking the word in season, speaking up for justice and Christian values. And then just being friends. Often friendship with us has to come first, before people are ready for friendship with God, with Jesus. Praying can help: 'Wrap N in your love'; 'Help me to love/tolerate N'; 'Forgive me for . . .'

Some people after a conversion experience are called out from their old places to new spheres of work and influence, possibly to undertake jobs directly linked to the Church's life and ministry, to local government, to work within a charity giving time voluntarily. Others will not be called away from their present work but continue where they are, perhaps with a new sense of presence. There is a Zen saying: 'How marvellous this, how mysterious! I chop wood, I draw water.' The same activities and duties are pursued after conversion as before, but now with a sense of wonder. The British Anglican devotional writer, Olive Wyon, described this new sense of divine presence:

> *To ears which have been trained to wait upon God in silence, and in*
> *the quietness of meditation and prayer, a very small incident, or a*
> *word, may prove to be a turning-point in our lives, and a new opening*
> *for his love to enter our world, to create and to redeem.*[10]

The 'heart's tooling'

Prayer, 'seeing' God in our daily lives, is no different from any other form of art or skill; it needs much practice and that means giving time to it. In a poem called *Emerging* R. S. Thomas, the Welsh Anglican priest-poet, writes of the 'heart's tooling', which is achieved 'little by little'. This 'heart's tooling' must surely be understood, whatever else it means, as a prayerful life, a contemplative regard. 'Contemplation' may seem a pretentious notion that can have little to do with ordinary daily life and a lot to do with life in a convent or monastery, a life removed from the pressures of 'ordinary' daily life.

Although it does have connotations of a certain kind of prayer, the grassroots of the word *templum* (temple) points to the creation of a sacred space or place in the here and now. We could go as far as to say that all the ingredients of our daily lives can become the building-blocks of a *templum*, a sacred space. Our inner eyes need training to see this. Apart from this general truth about our daily lives, we need to create a space, a *templum*, of time for direct communion with God, however small, within them. Some people find it helps to make a little *templum*, a shrine within the house somewhere, in which to focus during such a time.

A matter of time?

Our lives as human beings are no longer determined by the cycles of nature, the rhythms of the seasons, the stars and planets, but, seemingly exclusively, by the tempo of the modern world. Our culture tells us that time is money. As Jürgen Moltmann said, 'modern "homo accelerandus" (man-in-a-hurry) is cared for by McDonald's, poor guy! He has a great many encounters, but does not really experience anything, since although he wants to see everything, he internalizes nothing and reflects upon nothing'.[12]

It has been noted that we have more free time now than ever before yet never have we had so little time. Is 'life in the fast lane' humane and really worth living? Some top executives, we read, are giving up their 90-hour-a-week jobs so as to have more time for their families, for actually savouring life.

This work of the 'heart's tooling' requires some balance in our lives. There is a Hebrew tradition that says that God spends every 24 hours in this way: eight hours studying the Torah (devotion), eight hours administering the universe (work), eight hours playing with Leviathan (play/relaxation). That seems an appropriate model. Time features largely in our lives and there is one truth that applies to us all: we cannot change the past, and the future is not yet ours. We have only the present moment. It is there that God addresses us. God waits for us in this moment, whatever the moment holds. The consciousness of this reality can transform our work, our relationships, our lives.

Buddhists have a concept of mindfulness, attentiveness; when eating, eat, when walking, walk. Pay attention. The practice of breathing consciously and mindfully is counselled (as with the Jesus Prayer in the Christian tradition). This breathing can be a technique for becoming attentive and mindful, for living in the present moment: 'the only time to be alive is in the present moment, to be aware that we are here and now', to enjoy the present moment.[13] The eighteenth-century French Jesuit, Jean-Pierre de Caussade, writes in his book, *Self-Abandonment to Divine Providence*, of this precious present moment: 'What treasures of grace

lie concealed in these moments filled apparently by ordinary events . . . O Bread of Angels, heavenly manna, pearl
of the Gospel, sacrament of the present moment'.[14]

Arrow prayers

This attitude of attentiveness can be helped to grow
through the use of arrow prayers, prayed anywhere, any
time. Some people find the Jesus Prayer (beloved by the
Orthodox) very helpful: 'Lord Jesus Christ, Son of the
Living God, have mercy', or more shortly, 'Jesus, mercy',
or just, 'Jesus'. Or any words can be used. The four-
teenth-century English author of *The Cloud of Unknowing*
suggests the one word, 'God'.[15] We can make up our own
word, or phrase, or mantra – the psalms are full of them
– and offer the prayer while waiting at the bus-stop or for
the kettle to boil, the computer to fire up, the next client
to appear, in the traffic jam and throughout the day. If we
give time to these little prayers we shall find that they say
themselves in our depths when we are not particularly
thinking of them. We can, though, say them consciously
over everything: our feelings, over people, and the events
of the day.

Finally each evening we can gather up the 'manna' of the
day, seeing where God has been with us, discerning what
has been life-giving in work and relationships, and what has
not; what needs forgiveness; and the blessings that have
come to us.

Holy living

*God has given to us a short time here on earth, and yet upon this eter-
nity depends.*

*We must remember that the life of each of us may be so ordered,
and indeed must be, that it may be a perpetual serving of God. For
God provides the good things of the world to serve the needs of nature*

by the labours of the farmer, the skill and pains of the artisan, and the dangers and traffic of the merchant; these people and all of us, are in our different callings, the ministers of the Divine Providence, and the stewards of creation, servants of the great human family of God in all our work. In their own way also a monarch and priest, a judge and a lawyer ... are doing the work of God.

No one can complain that their calling takes them off from religion, for the calling itself and employment in honest trades and offices is a serving of God.[16]

Some questions

1 Where did you discern God in your workplace today?
2 Where did you discern God in your home today?
3 What is your greatest need? What is life-giving to you?

CHAPTER 9

The Call to Ministry

Peter Edwards

God calls us in all our variety, and in all our needs. God calls within the Church, and outside the Church. God knows our needs — and the needs of the Body of Christ throughout the world. In response to those needs many have felt a call to specific activity in the Church. This chapter explores the ways in which that might happen, and the questions you might need to ask yourself. We will be looking at the existing processes for accredited ministry: Church of England selection procedures are all under review at this time. On page 141 we offer contact addresses.

> For as in one body we have many members, and not all the members have the same function, so we, who are many, are one body in Christ, and individually we are members one of another. We have gifts that differ according to the grace given to us: prophecy, in proportion to faith; ministry, in ministering; the teacher, in teaching; the exhorter, in exhortation; the giver, in generosity; the leader, in diligence; the compassionate, in cheerfulness.
>
> Romans 12.4–8

Our earliest vocation was to know and love God. This fundamental calling probably occurred some time ago. Those with a lively vocation may be able to speak of their earliest awareness of being called in this way. In our response came the dawning of faith, a realization that we were indeed already in a living relationship with God. This brought with it the potential for reciprocating and seeking to know and do his will.

Having a sense of God's purpose for us in our lives is part of our vocation from God. Our vocation to faith, to service, to worship may have been heard through other people. There may have been significant individuals who helped to lead us on our journey, and the institutional or local Church may have been vitally important within this process.

We all have a story to tell of our awareness of vocation to living membership of the Church, and sharing such faith stories can be a real encouragement, to ourselves and also to others. Through telling and hearing these stories we will come to understand the always unique and yet strangely similar ways in which individual members of the Church have continuously experienced a vocation to active Christian faith and ministry, and how they have worked out how to respond.

Our role as members of the Church

All the baptized are members of the *laos*: the whole people of God. We are a 'royal priesthood', a 'holy nation', God's own, peculiar, people, set apart and dedicated for his own possession. The role of the Church in the world is to:

> *Offer spiritual sacrifices acceptable to God ... proclaim the mighty acts of him who called you out of darkness into his marvellous light.*
> 1 Peter 2.5b and 9b

The important principle here is that the Church itself has a ministry: the ministry of the whole people of God to participate in worship, service and mission. It is what the Church on earth is for, and it is what the Church is on earth for. Within that divinely established and led institution and community, there are also individual ministries for members.

Once we have found our feet within the life of the Church, we quickly recognize that there are those who seem to be part of a shared leadership, though that may not be quite how we express what we see. As newcomers, we perceive certain people each week 'doing' things. They are clearly established and respected members who have, it may seem, come to earn a place in the limelight. While it is fair to say that some ministries require a period of community stability from the individual, all the *laos* have both the gift from God of a ministry, and the potential for this to be developed within them. As we have read in Chapter Five, these gifts and ministries are allotted to each individual 'as the Spirit chooses' (1 Cor. 12.11). The Holy Spirit inspires the life, worship and mission of the Church, so it should come as no surprise that one of the missionary tasks of the Church and its leadership is to perceive, discern and develop the gifts of God in the members.

The conscious ministry of a Christian usually begins, therefore, within the life of the local church. There are those, however, who are not people of faith, or who are Christians in their hearts, who later come to a more developed faith as a result of somehow being called into the fellowship of the worshipping community. It is now that their previous good works begin to acquire a different meaning and focus. Serving Christ becomes more meaningful than simply serving my neighbour, though the two are one.

Our vocation almost certainly developed into understanding something of a personal ministry which will have been exercised in practical ways in our Christian lives. We might ask ourselves how our faith has changed, and how our ministry has grown and developed as we have lived within the faith community of the Church. We may realize that we have begun to see and hear things differently: indeed, that we have changed as people. This is something which others may have noticed, and which has affected how we feel about ourselves.

Within the life of the Church, we have probably taken on new responsibilities. Perhaps we volunteered, or maybe someone perceived that we had certain gifts, or maybe just some time to spare. Sometimes people are asked individually, or as part of a general appeal for help with particular ministries. Some are glad to be asked, but others shrink away from the challenge. Perhaps all that we needed was to be asked; or perhaps we required some encouragement or persuasion. Not everyone gives a positive response to all such requests, and we may have regrets at lost opportunities. Nevertheless, these have doubtless played a part in making us who we are today.

We are probably all well aware of the tasks that church members find themselves engaged in. There are ministries within worship, like reading, leading intercessions, serving, singing in the choir, helping with Sunday School. Then there are the ministries of serving on the PCC, or Deanery Synod; becoming a churchwarden, the incumbent's secretary, being on the cleaning or flower rota, or doing odd jobs in the maintenance of the church plant. It is very important not to underestimate the significance of engaging in any of these ministries. They mark defining moments in the development of vocation and response within the life of a Christian.

It happens all the time but it doesn't happen to everyone, and the reasons for this are worth thinking about. Perhaps there are willing and able people who are being overlooked by those in leadership roles. Some don't get asked or called and there are issues about how God, and the Church, ask and call people to particular ministries: about discernment of who is seen to be suitable; about gifts; about each person's potential; about the responsiveness of those who are approached.

One thing leads to another . . .
After I'd been at St Mary's for a few months, I agreed to help out with the Sunday School one day when they were short. Within two years I was in charge. I did the Bishop's Certificate in Sunday School work, really enjoyed it, and then the vicar asked if I would be interested in Reader Training. I did that, and served as a Reader for five years. Then the Church of England accepted that women could be priests, and that really made me think about my vocation. I decided to ask about it; one thing led to another, and next year I will be ordained.

The mature Christian is one who exercises a ministry within the Church and also in the world. Our desire to serve God will have changed the focus of our lives, at home, at work, at church. We may well have become more confident, even eager in our vocation to serve God in these ways, and recognize that we have something definite to offer, of which we were at one time unaware.

Authorized and accredited ministries

Within the life of the Church there is a variety of formally recognized accredited ministries, usually requiring some training and sometimes formal selection. These processes differ in the different Provinces of the Anglican Communion and are different in each denomination. Many dioceses encourage or require those pursuing a vocation to an authorized ministry to participate in some form of vocational guidance. Such schemes enable the concept of a developing vocation to be explored alongside others who have a similar sense of God wanting them to offer more of themselves in his service. Information about a range of ministries will be available, some of which are listed here.

The Reader

This is probably the longest-running formal, unpaid, lay ministry in the Church of England, open to men and women. Candidates may offer themselves, or may be called to the ministry by the incumbent, whose support, along with that of the PCC, is required prior to beginning training. This is particularly true if the training is to lead to admission as a Reader and active ministry within the home parish.

Readers are licensed to preach; to engage in a variety of instruction (initiation, confirmation, first communion, marriage, Bible study, prayer groups); to share in the leadership of worship; to conduct funerals; and to assist the local clergy as required. Training normally takes three years part-time, and funding is usually available from the PCC to meet the costs of the course. The nature of this training requires a degree of academic competence, as well as the agreement within the parish that the individual has other appropriate qualities to bring to this ministry. At the end of the course, the Bishop admits to the office of Reader those who will have a formal ministry within both the parish and the diocese.

Ministry teams

Individual dioceses have their own schemes for training for other ministries. Many encourage ministry teams to work in parishes alongside their clergy who train with them, learning new patterns of decision-making and sharing ministry with lay people. Some dioceses train people specifically for pastoral ministry, sharing the load of visiting and befriending. There are courses for those working with children and young people, and recognized training for full or part-time youth workers.

Hearing the call

When I first encountered a Reader, I wasn't quite sure who it was who was preaching one Sunday when I was on holiday and went to church. The priest was there in vestments, but then a woman wearing a blue preaching scarf ascended the pulpit steps. It was only on my return when I asked my own vicar what this meant that I realized this was a Reader. I had heard of this role, but had never encountered one before, and didn't think much about it until later on when I began to think about what it would be like to be able to preach. I realized that a parish priest often has to prepare more than one sermon each week, and that must be very time-consuming; and while our vicar usually preaches very well, it's nice to hear a different voice from time to time. I then asked him to tell me a bit more about what a Reader does, and we began to discuss the training required. I thought I might be able to help at Evensong, especially when he's away on holiday and it has to be cancelled, but I wasn't sure I would ever be able to write a sermon, let alone stand in the pulpit and deliver it. The important thing to remember is that training is designed to equip people for their ministry, and by the time I had done the three-year course, not only did I know a lot more about the Bible, I had become more confident about thinking things through theologically, and also about expressing my opinion in the seminar groups. I have been a Reader for three years now, and have helped with baptism and confirmation preparation groups, as well as leading Evensong about once a month, and preaching at the main Sunday Communion Service about once a month as well. I am now learning what to do in order to conduct a funeral. This feels rather daunting, as I won't know the people who are attending, but I am confident that I will be able to do this in due course. The best thing about my ministry is feeling that I am doing something challenging and rewarding, and offering some real help to our overworked vicar.

The Church Army

In addition to these, the work of the Church Army should be mentioned, in the selection, training, commissioning, deployment and support of those engaged in the specific ministry of an evangelist. This ministry is open to men and women alike, and is to be found in all parts of the Church of England, irrespective of a particular tradition. Training is usually residential over a three-year period, and equips the candidate for, usually, a full-time paid ministry combining a variety of elements according to the gifts of the individual officer. Areas of ministry include prisons, residential homes and hostels, contact with ex-offenders, young people and the elderly, and specific missionary enterprises. Some Church Army officers go on to become ordained, and may or may not retain their formal links with the organization.

Sharing ministry

When our last vicar retired, he was replaced by a much younger man who immediately started to suggest that lay people should share some of the responsibility for visiting the housebound, taking them Holy Communion, preparing wedding couples and confirmation candidates, as well as other areas of church life, such as the PCC. Many people felt that the elderly man had managed without all this help, so why did the young man need us to do what seemed to be his job? He then told a group of us that the diocese had suggested we might train together and form a parish ministry team, not simply to do his work, but to help us to understand more fully our own ministry as lay people, focused with particular shared responsibilities, and also to be able to keep parish life running when he might move on to another parish. We committed ourselves to a three-year stint on the team, during the course of which we would invite other members to join, shadowing our work, and then taking over from us one or two at a time over a period of about five years. By the end of this time, the team members had changed completely apart from the vicar who is still with us. Having finished my time on the team, I now have a better understanding of what kinds of skills are required for a range of ministries; I am able to give advice with the training of new members, and I am hoping I may be able to return to the team at some point in the future.

Spreading the word

When I went to university, I got involved with the Student Christian Fellowship, having been quite active in my home church. It was really good to meet with other, mainly young, Christians and to spread the word of the gospel within the context of the university. I wasn't at all sure what I wanted to do after graduation, so I took a gap year, and went to work in Kenya with a missionary society. Here, we lived and worked within a village community, and I began to think about what I would do on my return. It seemed to me that God was calling me to continue this kind of work, and I was really keen to carry on sharing my faith, and my interest in mechanical engineering. I trained for three years at the Church Army College, and was lucky enough to get a job in an industrial chaplaincy. Now I am able to help ordinary working people, most of whom are not churchgoers, to learn more about the Christian faith, just by meeting them in their workplace; and I also worship and am part of the leadership of a lively local church.

These ministries for lay people are all predominantly church-centred, though many contain elements of outreach to the local and wider community.

Religious communities

In a similar but different vein is the vocation to the religious life, a term which refers not just to the life of faith, but to those called to serve as friars, sisters, monks and nuns in a variety of religious houses and communities. Some of these will have been ordained as clergy prior to entering their community; others may find themselves called to the ordained life later on. A large number of religious, however, remain as lay people throughout their time, and serve the Church and the world according to the particular focus of the community of which they are members. Some communities are centred on a permanent life within their community house, rarely, if ever, stepping outside to the world for which they pray. Others are to be found working with church or other agencies. Most combine something of both, spending time working with local churches and projects, and returning to the community for periods of reflection, rest and the benefits of residential community life.

Call to community

For many years I was a wife and mother, working part-time in my local doctor's surgery. The children grew up and left home, and then a couple of years later my husband died quite suddenly. This left me feeling very vulnerable, and I became more actively involved in the life of my local church, where I had worshipped since the time of my husband's death and the funeral. This really was the turning point, when the priest had invited me to come to church, and I was made to feel welcome. We went on several occasions for quiet days at Nashdom Abbey, now closed. I had spent time talking with one of the monks, and each time we went, we would speak again. I loved the peace I experienced in that place, and the deep sense of prayer. I loved the worship, and the feeling of community as all the monks came from their work around the house and grounds to pray together through the day. It was a haven of Christian hospitality, and I missed it when I returned home. Eventually, I explored the possibility of spending some time in a women's religious community, and ended up with the Franciscans. There then followed times of extended retreat-cum-getting-to-know-you-and-us, with discussions about whether or not this would be the right move and the right kind of life for me. In the end, I joined the community as a postulant, served three years as a novice, and then took my life vows. In the years that I have been a Franciscan sister, I have found fulfilment in the community life, working and worshipping together. I have been able to serve elderly people within the house and within the wider community. I have found a new peace which I would barely have thought imaginable ten years ago, and I am still able to stay with and enjoy times with my children and boisterous grandchildren, returning, with gratitude, to the tranquillity of my, rather different, community family and home, and the security of the love of God and those with whom I now share my life.

Ordained ministry

A vocation to the ordained ministry may be experienced in a variety of ways, not least because there is a variety of ministries, as well as the different orders of the historic threefold ordained ministry of the Church: bishop, priest and deacon. It is, perhaps, unlikely that a priest might use this publication in seeking to discern a vocation to be a bishop, but the role of vocation in such a ministerial progression should not be entirely ignored. Ordained ministry is not superior to other ministries, but the process of discernment, selection and training is more testing and rigorous than for many other vocations and ministries. What is written here is, therefore, more detailed in its exploration of this particular vocation. It is intended to enable lay men and women who are at some stage of awareness of a vocation to ordination to focus on some of the personal qualities which are desirable in an ordained person. It deals also with the criteria expected by the Church of England's selection process, and it identifies the principal areas of ministry where the ordained person may be found.

The selection process

It is important to recognize that the selection of candidates for ordained ministry is a continuous process, which begins as soon as the individual becomes aware of a vocation. There is a degree of self-selection as the individual engages with the expectations and requirements. Discussion among family and friends will provide further encouragement or discouragement, and the individual's parish priest will develop the process by expressing pleasure and support, surprise and caution. It is worth saying that local clergy are encouraged to be as realistic and truthful as possible at this point. There is nothing to be gained by a parish priest passing the buck along the line of selection, where the individual is known less well as a whole person. It is far easier for a priest and a member of the congregation to work together through any negative issues at an early stage. Better this, than for the individual to have hopes and expectations raised only to see them crumble at a later stage.

Ordained Local Ministry

Having spent many years worshipping at the same church, serving on the PCC, reading the lessons and generally being part of the furniture, it came as a bit of a shock when our rector asked if I was likely to stay in the area when I retired from work in a couple of years, and wondered if I would think about the possibility of ordination. This eventually came about through the Diocesan Ordained Local Ministry scheme. He felt that it would be good to continue to have me as a friend and colleague, and that in the present climate of amalgamating parishes and spreading the stipendiary clergy more thinly, it would mean that St Mark's would be guaranteed someone to take the services, at least until I was too old to do so! The PCC were consulted, and then soundings were taken among the congregation. I went through a formal selection process, and I am currently two years into weekly evening classes arranged by the diocese. In a year's time I will be ordained as a deacon, and then in another year, as a priest. The course has been an eye-opener for me, as I have spent time in other parishes at weekends and on other occasions. It's been a long time since I did any serious study, but I have really enjoyed the course so far. What has really encouraged me has been the fact that my fellow church members have backed this idea right from the start; and it has also given me an amazing new beginning, doing something for the church — giving something back, that had never previously occurred to me to be possible.

If contact is made with the Diocesan Director of Ordinands (DDO) the process of selection becomes more

formal. Each diocese has its own policy for discerning vocations to ordained ministry, but there are broad similarities.
A candidate is likely to have a number of meetings with a
DDO, over several months or even years, during the course
of which the DDO will come to know more of the person,
who will be encouraged to provide evidence of a vocation
which is both authentic and realistic in its aspirations. The
DDO will have in mind the criteria agreed by the Ministry
Division of the Church of England, so that these may be
tested over a period of time within a developing and secure
relationship. At any point during these explorations, the
DDO may indicate that he or she is unable to affirm the
candidate's vocation any further. It may be that the candidate has also reached an awareness that this is the right decision. It is to be hoped that the two can reach agreement,
and it might be suggested that the candidate return to the
process at some later stage.

   If the process has developed positively, the DDO will ask
the candidate to meet with a bishop's examining chaplain,
who may be lay or ordained, in order to seek a second
opinion on the candidate's vocation. It may be that the
DDO has misgivings which will be endorsed by an impar-
tial adjudicator. The DDO may feel that this is a good candidate, whose progress towards a selection conference
requires the approval of the bishop's examiner. The DDO
and the examining chaplain will seek to reach agreement
on the candidate, and the process either stops there or
continues with a selection conference, where candidates
are observed during a two-day period, as well as under-
going formal interviews with the selectors, and engaging in
a range of exercises alongside other candidates.

   Throughout this entire process, those who have responsibility to discern and select will have in mind the fulfilment
of the following criteria. Some searching questions are
included, to enable readers to test their self-knowledge,
and perhaps to prepare for aspects of the selection process.

Selection criteria

Ministry within the Church of England
Candidates should be familiar with the tradition and practice of the Church of England, and be ready to work with them. These, or similar questions, need to be borne in mind:

- *What do you appreciate most about the Church of England?*
- *What is your experience and understanding of the different traditions within Anglicanism?*
- *What is a priest?*
- *What is your understanding of the representative nature of ordained ministry?*

Vocation
Candidates should be able to speak of their vocation to ministry and mission, referring both to their own conviction and to the extent to which others have confirmed it. Their sense of vocation should be obedient, realistic and informed.

- *How has your sense of vocation developed? What have been the milestones?*
- *Have other people helped you to come to an understanding of your vocation?*
- *What are your gifts and how could they be used in your vocation?*
- *How has your sense of vocation changed you as a person?*

Faith
Candidates should show an understanding of the Christian faith and a desire to deepen their understanding. They should demonstrate personal commitment to Christ, and a capacity to communicate the gospel.

- *What is your gospel? What is the heart of the good news you want to share?*
- *In among all that you believe about the Christian faith, what would you go to the stake for?*
- *What experiences in your life have strengthened or weakened your faith?*
- *What is faith and what is the opposite of faith?*

Spirituality

Candidates should show evidence of a commitment to a spiritual discipline, involving individual and corporate prayer and worship. Their spiritual practice should be such as to sustain and energize them in their daily lives.

- *What is your daily pattern of spirituality?*
- *How does your spirituality inform your life?*
- *Who is God for you? What kind of God do you relate to?*
- *Why pray?*

Personality and character

Candidates should be sufficiently mature and stable to show that they are able to sustain the demanding role of a minister, and to face change and pressure in a flexible and balanced way. They should be seen to be people of integrity.

- *Who do you say that you are?*
- *Who do others say that you are?*
- *What are your strengths and weaknesses?*
- *How well suited temperamentally are you to your vocation?*

Relationships
Candidates should demonstrate self-awareness and self-acceptance as a basis for developing open and healthy professional, personal and pastoral relationships as ministers. They should respect the teachings of the Church on matters of sexual morality.

How well do you relate to others?
- *What kind of people are you friendly with? Is there a pattern to your friendships?*
- *What kinds of people do you find difficult and why?*
- *What kind of relationships do you need to sustain you in your vocation?*

Leadership and collaboration
Candidates should show ability to offer leadership in the church community, and to some extent in the wider community. This ability includes the capacity to offer an example of faith and discipleship, to collaborate effectively with others, as well as to guide and shape the life of the church community in its mission to the world.

Stipendiary Ministry – Parochial, or sector: working as a paid employee of the Church but not in a parish context.

Non-stipendiary Ministry – Ministering, usually in the parish, but without financial return. In some dioceses these clergy are called Self-Supporting Ministers.

Ministry in Secular Employment – Being paid by a body other than the Church, either to minister primarily as a cleric, or in a way in which the clerical identity is on an equal footing with the professional identity, or perhaps not clearly visible.

Ordained Local Ministry – Working primarily within the home parish, or in other employment but serving the home parish with the expectation that this will remain the ministerial base for the long term.

- *What is your chosen leadership style?*
- *When you have exercised leadership, how have others responded?*
- *How good are you at working alongside and motivating others?*
- *In your experience of working with others, what have you found frustrating or stressful and why?*

Leadership, collaboration and the shape of ministry are subjects that many find it hard to talk about without fear of sounding pious, but candidates for ordination and, indeed, the clergy, need to be able confidently and humbly to do so.

Quality of mind
Candidates should have the necessary intellectual capacity and quality of mind to undertake satisfactorily a course of theological study and ministerial preparation, and to cope with the intellectual demands of ministry.

- *How best do your learn? Is it by listening, watching, reading or other ways?*
- *What books have you read which have excited you?*
- *What gets you thinking?*
- *What do you enjoy talking about?*

The outcome of the selection conference

Following attendance at a selection conference the candidates leave and the selectors remain to fulfil their deliberations and to reach agreement about each of the candidates:

whether or not to recommend them to their diocesan Bishop for ordination training.

It is important to remember that the recommendation, or not, is made by the selectors to the diocesan Bishop, who will make the final decision about the candidate. This will be conveyed to the candidate, either in person or by letter, by the Bishop or by the DDO. In practice, the majority of Bishops uphold the decision of the selectors, although there are a small number of occasions when, for a particular reason, a candidate may proceed towards further training despite not being recommended by the selectors.

Whatever the outcome, the candidate will meet with the DDO in order to discuss the selectors' report. This, and the availability of further support, is particularly important to enable those not recommended as ordinands to come to terms with the decision that has been made. Candidates who have not been recommended may experience many emotions, not least a sense of loss or bereavement. It will be important to recognize that these Christians still have a vocation and ministry, but that the Church has not been able to recognize at this stage the validity of the call to ordained ministry.

For those who are recommended, and are sponsored by their Bishop and diocese for further training, the rush of pleasure and excitement can often be succeeded by feelings of panic. This will be a life-changing experience, through the demands of making plans for courses or colleges, embarking on that period of training and study, preparing for ordination and establishing a parish-base for future ministry. At the end of it all, there will be the gift of a new ministry at ordination, and then the learning really begins!

But if you are in doubt how you may best lay out your life, and if you are quite clear in your acceptance of Jesus Christ as your Saviour and your God, then the mere circumstances of the time constitute a call to the Church's direct service in its ministry which you must face; for there is no sphere of life in which you can more certainly lay out all your talents in the service of God. It will call for every capacity; it will bring you into touch with human beings in every conceivable relation. There is no life so rich or so full of all those joys which come from serving people at the point of their greatest need.[1]

CHAPTER 10

The Call to Continue

Stephen Ferns

In the first chapter we saw that God's calling began before time. It is true to say that this call never ends. We are all called into a relationship that never ceases. We learn from God and from each other what our calling is. Discerning that call to us is not a one-off: God's calling continues throughout our lives as we are given opportunities to respond to God's will for us and so to grow in grace.

One of the difficulties with vocational language is the kind of expectations with which it is loaded. Having a vocation is still commonly perceived as wishing to be ordained or to enter a religious community. Moreover, because vocation is tied up with the priestly or religious life, to have a vocation implies a life-long commitment which is consistent and unchanging. However, this chapter will argue for a different way of approaching vocation. As we have seen, having a vocation is not the preserve of priests, monks and nuns: all of us as people of God have a vocation. The word 'vocation' is used in the singular but it would be more accurate to say that all of us have vocations in the plural. Our vocations change during the course of our lives. We are called to do different things and to be different people as we are exposed to new situations and circumstances. Our vocations grow and develop as we grow and develop. Consequently, what we perceived to be our calling at 18 may be very different from how we perceive our calling at 50. The vocational chapter of our lives is never completed. Our vocation is ongoing and continuous.

A growing vocation

To talk about having a vocation suggests that we are committing ourselves to a way of being, which will shape and mould our lives. Although our vocations will differ from one another, and we will experience a variety of vocations during the course of our life, there will nevertheless be a common denominator running through those different vocations: we are each called to be Christ's, and to live out our lives in response to his life, death and resurrection.

> *A service which involves emptying oneself and working for the good of others is at the very heart of the Christian vocation. The followers of Christ do not seek power and riches in order to manipulate other human beings and beggar the earth. Rather they hear the call, 'If any want to become my followers, let them deny themselves and take up their cross daily and follow me.'*[1]

One of the most popular devotional books is *The Imitation of Christ* by Thomas à Kempis. The book has dozens of short chapters on different aspects of the life of Christ. The central insight of the book is that in the Christian life it is possible for us to imitate the life of Christ. Our task as Christians is to replicate Christ's life here on earth. The way to do that is to work through a long check-list of the virtues and attributes of Christ and to see where we are on target and where we are falling short. It seems like a splendid ideal and an attractive model for the Christian life. However, the question is: How realistic is it?

Being ourselves

Becoming like Christ in every detail is not a live option for us. In Christ, we see what it means to be truly human and truly divine. The incarnation teaches us that Christ is unique:

there can never be an exact copy of Christ again in the world. Even the saints, the most holy men and women of every generation, are not carbon copies of Christ. Rather, they have entered into the family likeness of Christ. Within their lives we can glimpse a particular aspect of Christ's life: there will be a particular image of Christ that will have sparked their imagination, a particular image they will have been drawn to, a particular image that it has been possible for them, given their own personalities and gifts and circumstances, to replicate in their own lives. For St Antony of Egypt, it was the image of Christ going into the desert to pray. For St Francis of Assisi, it was the image of Christ as the man of humility and poverty. For Charles de Foucauld it was the image of Christ living anonymously during the hidden years in Nazareth. For Mother Teresa it was the image of the vulnerable Christ to be found in the hungry and the naked and the sick.

Being Christ-like does not involve us in a personality transplant. Rather, being Christ-like involves discovering what aspect of the life of Christ we are drawn to and what aspect of the life of Christ we can realistically and gracefully develop within our lives. Being Christ-like is not about being something or someone we are not; being rooted in service, however, is an integral part of the Christian vocation, as Albert Schweitzer recognized:

> I don't know what your destiny will be, but one thing I know, the only ones among you who will be really happy are those who have sought and found how to serve.[2]

Who are you?

One of the central questions in the Gospels is Jesus' question to his disciples, 'But who do you say that I am?' (Mark 8.29). It is a question which is not primarily an invitation

to theological speculation; it is a practical question at the
heart of the Christian calling. Who is Jesus for you? What
attracts you to him? What aspect of his life and personality
could you realistically reflect within yours? Furthermore,
Christ's question: 'Who do you say that I am?' is actually
linked to another question: 'Who do you say that you are?'
What kind of people are we and what kind of people do we
have the capability of being and becoming?

Who we are, and who we recognize Jesus to be, is at the
heart of the response to our ongoing and continuous
calling. Being Christ's is the common denominator that
runs through our common calling as Christian disciples.
But how we work that out in practice will depend very
much upon what is possible for us given our own personalities and gifts. We are called to be truly ourselves and by
being truly ourselves, our best selves, we end up reflecting
something of the nature of Christ.

Why are we called?

Part of living out this vocation of being Christ's is to recognize the importance of why we are being called for this
purpose. The reason is clear and straightforward: our
calling as Christians is to continue God's work in Christ of
reconciling the world to himself; our mission in Christ is to
continue the work of the incarnation. St Teresa of Avila
expressed this in characteristic, down-to-earth, style when
she wrote:

> Christ has no body now on earth but yours,
> no hands but yours, no feet but yours;
> yours are the eyes through which is to look out
> Christ's compassion to the world,
> yours are the feet with which he is to go about doing good,
> and yours are the hands with which he is to bless us now.[3]

Suddenly our vocation to be Christ's takes on a sharper focus. We are the co-workers of God, doing what we can to discern the movement of the Spirit in the world around us and trying to co-operate with the Spirit in the fulfilment of God's will.

Expressed like that, our vocation has less to do with our role within the life of the Church, whether we are lay or ordained. It is more to do with the Kingdom of God – that time and space where God is God, and everyone and everything is in union with God. It is ensuring that we ourselves are signs of the Kingdom and that we give over our lives to working for supporting the values of the Kingdom.

This vocation is lived out in the world. Sometimes we make the mistake of being so Church-centred, we assume that the Church, rather than the world, is the arena for God's presence and activity. The truth is that God is to be found in the world, often hidden and anonymous, reconciling the whole of creation to himself. The world is where we encounter God and where we have opportunities to discern God's will and co-operate with his Spirit. But how do we do that? How do we discern God's call to us and how do we co-operate with his Spirit?

Being in the world

For us to be open to the movement of God's Spirit within the world, we have to be open to the movement of God's Spirit within ourselves. We will be disciplined in our times of prayer and in those times of prayer we will wait upon God's presence, silently in expectation. The story is told of Michael Ramsey, the former Archbishop of Canterbury, being asked by a student how long he prayed for each day. He replied, 'Five minutes.' 'That's not very long,' retorted the student. The Archbishop replied, 'I spend five minutes in prayer and two hours preparing for those five minutes.' The quality of our prayer is important and we need to be generous in the amount of time we give to it. Our time of prayer opens us up to God's working within us. We are touched by God's presence and begin the process of learning what it might be to dance in tune with the Spirit.

Alive to God

As our life of prayer grows, so we discover two other developments. First, the scriptures, particularly the Gospels, become increasingly important to us. They become alive with the presence of God and speak to us in a way that is profound and exciting. The Gospel stories, which may in the past have seemed not altogether relevant to us, take on a new life and we begin to see ourselves within the stories and find ourselves encountering the living Christ through them. We begin to appreciate ever more profoundly what Christ is like, what is important to him and how he transforms the individuals and situations with which he has contact. Through the scriptures we begin to recognize who Christ is. The second development is equally striking. Having encountered the living Christ in the scriptures, we begin to see him in the world around us, in other people, in situations, in creation. Suddenly, in the poet Gerard Manley Hopkins' words, 'The world is charged with the grandeur of God'.[4]

Alive to others

However, being alive to God's presence within the world also has the effect of making us sensitive to people or situations where there is suffering or exploitation or wickedness. We sense God's suffering in the midst of his creation and we recognize our own calling to bring light into dark places, to bring hope where there is despair, to bring life where there is death. Our ongoing vocation is to struggle for peace and justice within the world whether it be situations we ourselves encounter, or situations we read about in our newspapers and watch on our televisions. The nightly television news becomes less of a matter of entertaining viewing or an opportunity to bring ourselves up-to-date with world events, than a channel by which God calls us to action in working for the Kingdom. Meister Eckhart believed that it is our 'sharing' of God's nature that sanctifies the work we do in the world:

> People ought not to consider so much what they are to do as what they are; let them but be good and their ways and deeds will shine brightly. If you are just, your actions will be just too. Do not think that saintliness comes from occupation; it depends rather on what one is. The kind of work we do does not make us holy but we may make it holy. However 'sacred' a calling may be, as it is a calling, it has no power to sanctify; but rather as we are and have the divine being within, we bless each task we do, be it eating, or sleeping, or watching, or any other. Whatever they do, who have not much of [God's] nature, they work in vain. [5]

Alive to ourselves

So we try to be alert and awake to God's action in the world and try to respond to our calling as his co-workers in Christ in reconciling the world to himself. But included in God's action in the world is God's action within us as he reconciles us to himself. If we are to open ourselves to the movement of the Spirit, we will become aware that every moment is an opportunity for grace. The present moment, to use the words of the French spiritual writer Jean-Pierre de Caussade, is sacramental. Consequently, each moment of our day becomes precious as an opportunity, in our daily decision-making, to work with the Spirit. Sometimes the decisions will be momentous with far-reaching implications and effects. For the most part, the decisions we take are small and seem insignificant but actually may have all sorts of ramifications for people we do not know in parts of the world we have never visited. Deciding which brand of coffee to buy may seem trivial, but whether we go for a brand which is fairly traded or a brand which exploits its workers in the developing world will affect people's lives.

How can we know?

How do we know that our decision-making is in accord with God's will? The insights of St Ignatius Loyola are particularly helpful in the process of the discernment of spirits. St Ignatius taught that as we choose a particular course of action, we should try and discern how it makes us feel. Does it fill us with a sense of joy, peace and consolation or does it make us feel ill at ease, restless and disconsolate? Sometimes we need to monitor our feelings over time since a decision which initially brings us a sense of peace can in time make us feel deeply uneasy. For Ignatius, knowing our true self and knowing God are closely interlinked. If our lives are orientated towards God, he will reveal his will to us and we will increasingly learn what brings us close to God's presence and what draws us away from that presence. We begin to recognize that God is calling us to be Christ's in each moment of each day: a call to co-operate with the Spirit in the big and little things of life as we all work together for the Kingdom.

Vocation, our calling in Christ, is not an optional extra for those considering ordination or the religious life. It is at the heart of what it is to live out an authentic Christian life. It is closely linked to prayer because it is about responding to God's activity in today's world and to be able to co-operate with God's Spirit we need to stay close to, and be able to recognize, the movements of the Spirit. Our calling may involve us in major decisions and change. We may experience callings of the kind that we read in the scriptures where people like Abraham have their lives turned upside-down as they respond to God's call to them. However, for the most part, we will probably experience God's call in listening to his voice every day and trying to discern in each present moment what it is that God requires of us. That sense of calling may be less earth-shattering than Abraham's calling, but in the long term it may turn our lives upside-down just as much as Abraham's call turned his life upside-down. Our calling to be Christ's is continuous and ongoing, and through it God will help us to become our best selves for his glory, and for the furtherance of his Kingdom. *This Is Our Calling.*

Some questions

1 How has your sense of vocation changed during different periods of your life?
2 What is God calling you to be and to do now? How do you know?
3 What is the purpose of your calling?

Notes

Introduction

1 *This Is Our Faith*, ed. Jeffrey John (Chawton: Redemptorist Publications, 1995).
2 A prayer of Thomas Merton from *Thoughts in Solitude* (New York: Farrer, Straus & Giroux, 1958), p. 83 (adapted).

1 The Call through Creation

1 Rowan Williams, 'Vocation' (published by the Vocations Team, Society of St Francis, The Friary, Hilfield, Dorchester, Dorset DT2 7BE), p. 4. The article first appeared in *Encounter and Exchange*.
2 *The Book of Common Prayer and Administration of the Sacraments and Other Rites and Ceremonies of the Church* according to the use of the Episcopal Church of the USA.
3 Rowan Williams, 'Vocation', p. 4.
4 Daniel O'Leary, *New Hearts, New Models: Spirituality for Priests* (New York: Columba Press, 1997), p. 35.
5 *A Kierkegaard Anthology*, ed. Robert Bretail (Princeton, NJ: Princeton University Press, 1946), pp. 4–5.
6 Rainer Maria Rilke, *Letters to a Young Poet*, tr. Stephen Mitchell (New York: Random House, 1984), p. 34.

3 The Call for Others

1 St Bernard of Clairvaux, from Homily 4, 8–9, in *From the Fathers to the Churches*, ed. Br Kenneth, CGA (Glasgow: Collins, 1983).
2 From Sermon 10 in Michael Stancliffe's *Symbols and Dances* (London: SPCK, 1986).
3 Stancliffe, *Symbols*, Sermon 10.

5 The Call of Disciples

1 A. T. Hanson, cited in C. Rowland, *Christian Origins* (London: SPCK, 1989), p. 258.
2 Henri Nouwen, *The Wounded Healer* (London: Darton, Longman & Todd, 1994).

6 The Call through Baptism

1 *On the Way* (London: Church House Publishing, 1995; reprinted 1998), p. 39.
2 *Common Worship Initiation Services* (London: Church House Publishing, 1998), Holy Baptism, p. 27.

7 The Calling of the Church

1 Irenaeus of Lyons, *Against Heresies*, Book 3, 24.10: *Patrologia Graeca* 7–1 1037.

8 The Call to Pray and Work

1 Irenaeus of Lyons, *Against Heresies*, Book 4, 20.7: Patrologia Graeca 7–1 1037; also see *Early Church Fathers* (Irenaeus of Lyons), ed. R. M. Grant (London: Routledge, 1997).
2 Jürgen Moltmann, 'Preparing for the Third Millennium', lecture given at St Paul's Cathedral, London, September 1998.

3 Anthony de Mello in *The Song of the Bird* (New York: Doubleday, 1984), p. 12.

4 The Gospel of Thomas (Coptic text) in *The Apocryphal New Testament: A Collection of Apocryphal Christian Literature in English*. Translation based on M. R. James, ed. J. K. Elliott (Oxford: Oxford University Press, 1993), p. 144.

5 See, for example, *The Intimate Merton: The Life of Thomas Merton from his Journals*, ed. Patrick Hart and Jonathan Montaldo (Oxford: Lion, 2000), pp. 261–326.

6 *George Herbert: The Country Parson; The Temple*, ed. John N. Wall, Classics of Western Spirituality (New York: Paulist Press, 1981), *The Elixir*, p. 311.

7 Sir Jacob Astley (1579–1652), prayer before the Battle of Edgehill, in Sir Philip Warwick, *Memoires* (1701), p. 229; see *Oxford Dictionary of Quotations*, revised fourth edn 1996, p. 32.

8 John O'Donohue, *Anam Cara* (London: Bantam Press, 1997), p. 167; the prayer translated by Kuno Meyer.

9 Pierre Teilhard de Chardin, *Le Milieu Divin* (an essay on the interior life) (London: Collins, 1957), pp. 36f.

10 Olive Wyon, in *The Lion Christian Quotation Collection*, compiled by Hannah Ward and Jennifer Wild (Oxford: Lion, 2002), 20.599, no. 2, p. 332.

11 R. S. Thomas, *Later Poems 1972–1982* (London: Papermac, 1984), p. 117.

12 Moltmann, 'Preparing for the Third Millennium'.

13 Thich Nhat Hanh, *Living Buddha, Living Christ* (London: Rider, 1995), pp. 15ff.

14 Jean-Pierre de Caussade, SJ, *Self-Abandonment to Divine Providence*, tr. from the French by Algar Thorold (London: Burns & Oates, 1959), p. 5.

15 *The Cloud of Unknowing*, tr. Clifton Wolters, (London: Penguin Books, 1961), p. 61.

16 Jeremy Taylor, *Holy Living*, in William G. D. Sykes, *Visions of Faith* (London: Marshall Pickering, 1986), p. 395 (adapted).

9   The Call to Ministry

1   William Temple, *Christian Faith and Life* (London: SCM, 1963), p. 139; reprinted in William G. D. Sykes, *Visions of Faith* (London: Marshall Pickering, 1986), p. 395 (adapted).

10   The Call to Continue

1   Sean McDonagh, SSC, *The Greening of the Church* (London: Cassell, 1990); reprinted in Daniel P. Cronin, *Words of Encouragement* (New York: St Paul Publications, 1992), p. 150 (adapted).
2   Albert Schweitzer, in Cronin, *Words of Encouragement*, p. 150.
3   St Teresa of Avila, in *A Manual of Anglo-Catholic Devotion*, compiled by Andrew Burnham (Norwich: Canterbury Press Norwich, 2001), p. 65.
4   *God's Grandeur*, in *Flowers of Heaven: One Thousand Years of Christian Verse*, compiled by Joseph Pearce (London: Hodder & Stoughton, 2000).
5   Meister Eckhart, *Meister Eckhart*, tr. Raymond B. Blakney, (New York: Harper & Row, 1941), p. 6; reprinted in William G. D. Sykes, *Visions of Faith* (London: Marshall Pickering, 1986), p. 396.

Reading List

Vocation

John Adair: *How to Find your Vocation* (Canterbury Press Norwich, 2000)
Maria Boulding: *A Touch of God* (Triangle, 1988)
Stuart Buchanan: *On Call* (The Bible Reading Fellowship, 2001)
Os Clarke: *The Call* (Spring Harvest, 2001)
Francis Dewar: *Called or Collared* (new edition SPCK, 2000)
Francis Dewar: *Invitations: God's Calling for Everyone* (SPCK, 1996)
Francis Dewar: *Live for a Change* (DLT, 1988)
Henri Nouwen: *The Road to Daybreak* (DLT, 1997)

Ordained ministry

Liz and Andrew Barr: *Jobs for the Boys? Women Who Became Priests* (Hodder & Stoughton, 2001)
Andrew Bowden and Michael West: *Dynamic Local Ministry* (Continuum, 2000)
Michael Bowering (ed.): *Priesthood Here and Now* (Diocese of Newcastle, 1994)
Wesley Carr: *The Priestlike Task* (SPCK, 1985)
Andrew Clitherow: *Into Your Hands* (SPCK, 2001)
Jim Cotter: *Yes Minister* (Cairns, 1992)
William Countryman: *Living on the Border of the Holy: Renewing the Priesthood of All* (Morehouse Publishing, 1999)
Steven Croft: *Ministry in Three Dimensions* (DLT, 1999)
James M. Francis and Leslie J. Francis: *Tentmaking:*

Perspectives on Self-Supporting Ministry (Gracewing, 1998)

John Fuller and Patrick Vaughan (eds): *Working for the Kingdom* (SPCK, 1986)

Robin Greenwood: *Transforming Church* (SPCK, 2002)

Robin Greenwood: *Transforming Priesthood: A New Theology of Mission and Ministry* (SPCK, 2000)

Adey Grummet: S*uddenly He Thinks He's a Sunbeam* (SPCK/ Triangle, 2000)

George Guiver (ed.): *Priests in a People's Church* (SPCK, 2001)

George Guiver (ed.): *The Fire and the Clay* (SPCK, 1993)

Rod Hacking: *On the Boundary* (Canterbury Press Norwich, 1994)

Christine Hall and Robert Hannaford (eds): *Order and Ministry* (Gracewing, 1996)

Michael Hollings: *Living Priesthood* (McCrimmon, 1994)

Basil Hume: *Light in the Lord: Reflections on Priesthood* (St Paul's Publications, 1991)

Gordon Kuhrt: *An Introduction to Christian Ministry* (CHP, 2000)

Giles Legood: *Chaplaincy* (Continuum, 1999)

Christopher Moody: *Eccentric Ministry* (DLT, 1992)

Michael Ramsey: *The Christian Priest Today* (SPCK, 1999)

Alastair Redfern: *Ministry and Priesthood* (DLT, 1999)

Anthony Russell: *The Clerical Profession* (SPCK, 1980)

W. H. Vanstone: *Fare Well in Christ* (DLT, 1997)

W. H. Vanstone: *Love's Endeavour, Love's Expense* (DLT, 1978)

Anglicanism

Paul Avis: *The Anglican Understanding of the Church: An Introduction* (SPCK, 2000)

David L. Edwards: *What Anglicans Believe in the Twenty-first Century* (Continuum, 2002)

Monica Furlong: *C of E: The State It's In* (Hodder & Stoughton, 2000)

Richard Giles: *We Do Not Presume* (Canterbury Press Norwich, 1998)

Alastair Redfern: *Being Anglican* (DLT, 2000)

Stephen Sykes: *The Integrity of Anglicanism* (SPCK, 1978)

Stephen Sykes: *Unashamed Anglicanism* (DLT, 1995)

Religious life

Anglican Religious Communities Year Book (Canterbury Press Norwich, annually)

Sr Agatha Mary, SPB: *Rule of St Augustine* (Augustinian Press, 1991)

Dietrich Bonhoeffer: *Life Together* (SCM, 1954)

Barbara Fiand: *Refocusing the Vision: Religious Life into the Future* (The Crossroad Publishing Co., 2001)

Basil Hume, OSB: *Searching for God* (Gracewing, 2002)

Isabel Losada: *New Habits* (Hodder & Stoughton, 1999)

Mary Loudon: *Unveiled: Nuns Talking* (Ebury/Vintage, 1993)

Sr Mary Edna: *Religious Life* (Penguin, 1968)

Diarmuid O'Murchu, MSC: *Reframing Religious Life: An Expanded Vision for the Future* (St Paul's Publications, 1998)

David Parry, OSB: *The Household of God* (DLT, 1980)

David Parry, OSB: *The Rule of St Benedict* (DLT, 1984)

Timothy Radcliffe, OP: *Sing a New Song – The Christian Vocation* (Dominican Publications, 1999)

Sandra M. Schneiders, IHM: *Finding the Treasure* (Paulist Press, 2000)

Sandra M. Schneiders, IHM: *Selling All* (Paulist Press, 2001)

Jean Vanier: *Community and Growth: Our Pilgrimage Together* (DLT, 1989)

Spirituality

Angela Ashwin: *Heaven In Ordinary* (McCrimmon, 1985)

Maria Boulding: *The Coming of God* (Canterbury Press Norwich, 2001)

Ruth Burrows: *Before the Living God* (Sheed & Ward, 1979)

Lavinia Byrne: *Women Before God* (SPCK, 1995)

Stephen Cottrell: *Praying Through Life* (Church House Publishing, 1998)

Bruce Duncan: *Pray Your Way* (DLT, 1993)

Michael Paul Gallagher: *Letters on Prayer* (DLT, 1994)

Margaret Hebblethwaite: *Motherhood and God* (Continuum, 1984)

Margaret Hebblethwaite: *Finding God in All Things* (HarperCollins, 1987)

Joyce Huggett: *Learning the Language of Prayer* (The Bible Reading Fellowship, 1996)

Joyce Huggett: *Listening To God* (Hodder & Stoughton, 1996)

Joyce Huggett: *Open To God* (Eagle Publishing, 1997)

Gerard Hughes: *God of Surprises* (DLT, 1996)

Gerard Hughes: *God, Where Are You?* (DLT, 1997)

Gerard Hughes: *Oh God, Why?* (DLT, 2000)

William Johnston: *Arise My Love: Mysticism for a New Era* (Orbis Books, 2000)

William Johnston: *Being in Love: The Practice of Christian Prayer* (Fordham University Press, 1999)

Mother Mary Clare, SLG: *Encountering the Depths* (SLG Press, 1993)

Melvyn Matthews: *Both Alike to Thee: The Retrieval of the Mystical Way* (SPCK, 2000)

Donald Nicholl: *Holiness* (DLT, 1981)

Henri Nouwen: *The Return of the Prodigal Son* (DLT, 1994)

Joyce Rupp: *Dear Heart, Come Home* (The Crossroad Publishing Company, 1959)

Joyce Rupp: *May I Have This Dance?* (Ave Maria Press, 1992)

Philip Sheldrake (ed.): *Traditions in Christian Spirituality Series* (DLT)

Margaret Silf: *Landmarks – An Ignatian Journey* (DLT, 1998)

Margaret Silf: *Wayfaring* (DLT, 2001)

Ann Belford Ulanov and Barry Ulanov: *Primary Speech: A Psychology of Prayer* (John Knox Press, 1988)
John Wilkins (ed.): *How I Pray* (DLT, 1993)
Rowan Williams: *The Wound of Knowledge* (DLT, 1990)

Christian faith and theology

David Ford: *Theology: A Very Short Introduction* (OUP, 2000)
Anthony Hanson and Richard Hanson: *Reasonable Belief* (OUP, 1981)
Alister McGrath: *Christian Theology: An Introduction* (Blackwell, 2001)
Keith Ward: *Christianity: A Short Introduction* (SPCK, 2000)
Rowan Williams: *Lost Icons* (T & T Clark, 2000)
Rowan Williams: *On Christian Theology* (Blackwell, 1999)
Rowan Williams: *Open to Judgement* (DLT, 1994)

Self-knowledge and pastoral relationships

Alastair Campbell: *Rediscovering Pastoral Care* (DLT, 1986)
Wesley Carr: *Handbook of Pastoral Studies* (SPCK, 1997)
Malcolm Goldsmith and Martin Wharton: *Knowing Me Knowing You* (SPCK, 1993)
Gordon H. Jeff: *Spiritual Direction for Every Christian* (SPCK, 1987)
Henri Nouwen: *Compassion* (DLT, 1982)
Henri Nouwen: *The Wounded Healer* (DLT, 1994)
Philip Sheldrake: *Befriending Our Desires* (DLT, 1997)

Novels with theological themes

The list below provides some titles of novels exploring theological themes. The list is far from exhaustive.

Saul Bellow: *Henderson the Rain King* (Penguin Books, 2000)

Georges Bernanos: *The Diary of a Country Priest* (Carroll & Graf Publishers, 2002)

Margaret Craven: *I Heard the Owl Call My Name* (Pan Macmillan, 1980)

Fyodor Dostoyevsky: *The Brothers Karamazov* (Penguin Books, 1993)

Shasuko Endo: *Silence* (Peter Owen, 1996)

Catherine Fox: *Angels and Men* (Penguin Books, 1997)

Rumer Godden: *In This House of Brede* (Pan Macmillan, 1994)

Gail Godwin: *Father Melancholy's Daughter* (Avon Books, 1997)

William Golding: *Darkness Visible* (Faber & Faber, 1979)

William Golding: *Rites of Passage* (Faber & Faber, 1997)

William Golding: *The Spire* (Faber & Faber, 1997)

Graham Greene: *A Burnt-out Case* (Vintage/Ebury, 2001)

Graham Greene: *Monsignor Quixote* (Vintage/Ebury, 2000)

Graham Greene: *The Power and the Glory* (Vintage/Ebury, 2001)

Hermann Hesse: *Narcissus and Goldmund* (Peter Owen Publishers, 1999)

Herman Hesse: *Siddhartha* (Penguin Books, 1991)

Susan Hill: *In the Springtime of the Year* (Penguin Books, 1977)

Susan Howatch: *Glittering Images* (HarperCollins, 1996)

P. D. James: *Death in Holy Orders* (Faber & Faber, 2001)

P. D. James: *The Children of Men* (Faber & Faber, 2000)

David Lodge: *Therapy* (Penguin Books, 1996)

Sara Maitland: *Brittle Joys* (Virago Press, 2000)

Brian Moore: *Black Robe* (HarperCollins, 1987)

Brian Moore: *The Statement* (Plume Books, 1997)

Iris Murdoch: *The Bell* (Vintage/Ebury, 1999)

Barbara Pym: *A Glass of Blessings* (Pan Macmillan, 1994)

Salley Vickers: *Miss Garnet's Angel* (HarperCollins, 2000)

Morris West: *Eminence* (Harcourt, 1998)

Morris West: *Lazarus* (Arrow, 1995)

Morris West: *Shoes of the Fisherman* (Buccaneer Books, 1993)

Morris West: *The Clowns of God* (Hodder & Stoughton, 1989)

Morris West: *The Devil's Advocate* (Arrow, 1996)

Contact Addresses

The Vocations Officer
Ministry Division
Church House
Great Smith Street
London SW1P 3NZ
Website: www.cofe-ministry.org.uk

Anglican Religious Communities
Church House
Great Smith Street
London SW1P 3NZ
Website: www.orders.anglican.org/arcyb/

Central Readers' Council
Church House
Great Smith Street
London SW1P 3NZ
Website: www.ampleforth.u-net.com/crc/

Christians Abroad
Room 237 Bon Marché Centre
241–251 Ferndale Road
London SW9 8BJ
Website: www.cabroad.org.uk

Church Army
Candidates and Vocations Department
Church Army
Marlowe House
109 Station Road
Sidcup
Kent DA15 7AD
Website: www.churcharmy.org.uk

Affirming Catholicism
The Vocations Officer
Affirming Catholicism
St Matthew's House
20 Great Peter Street
London SW1P 2BU
Website: www.affirmingcatholicism.org.uk

Society of Catholic Priests
The Vocations Officer
Society of Catholic Priests
c/o Affirming Catholicism
St Matthew's House
20 Great Peter Street
London SW1P 2BU
Website: www.soccathpriest.org